The Clown Doctor Chronicles

D1572484

The Clown Doctor Chronicles

by

Caroline Simonds
&
Bernie Warren

Amsterdam – New York, NY 2004

The paper on which this book is printed meets the requirements of "ISO 9706:1994, Information and documentation – Paper of documents – Requirements for permanence".

ISBN: 90-420-1079-7
©Editions Rodopi B.V., Amsterdam – New York, NY 2004
Printed in The Netherlands

Acknowledgements

This book could not have been written without the assistance and kindness of many people and organisations.

First, a special thank you to Sharron Taylor, Office Manager for Fools for Health, for the many hours spent working on the technical details of the style sheet and text. Thank you also to Rob Fisher, Series Editor of *At the Interface and Probing the Boundaries* and to Eric van Broekhuizen at Rodopi for encouraging the English language version of this book. Special mention should go to Alora for her wonderful drawings and to Edyta Eansor and Dr Don Rudzinski for the Fools for Health photographs. Sidonie Loiseleux is gratefully acknowledged for the picture of Caroline in clown mode.

Both of us are borderline "workaholics." Finding time to write has been a struggle. Mainly we squeezed an hour here and an afternoon there into our busy professional and personal lives. However we were fortunate to have been awarded two writing residencies, one at *La Napoule Art Foundation* and another at *La Fondation des Treilles*. We are deeply indebted to these organisations and all of their staff for providing the solitude and space in which we were able to write without interruption or pressure.

We want to show gratitude to our families (Patrick and Lailah, Julie and Alora) who were unbelievably generous and understanding about our absences from home and our need to write at all hours when we were there!

Our applause continues with:

The administrative staff, board of directors and all the clowns of L.R.M. (past and present); Not to forget: Manu Bosc; Michael Christensen; Caroline Elliacheff; Laura Fernandez; Benedicte Guichardon; Martin Guichardon; Helen Hansen; Diana Mady Kelly; Nadine Nimier; Marie Nimier; Evelyne and Jacques Perrot; Donna Ryder; Stephen Ringold; Wellington Santos; Peter Senior; University of Windsor; Anne Vissuzaine; Kim Winslow; The Ministry of Culture, La Fondtion de France; The Florence Gould Foundation (John and Mary Young); Air France; Mamie Confiture; Plus all the corporate sponsors that have helped Le Rire Medecin survive over the years. To name only a few: U.P.S.A-B.M.S.; Cetelem; La Ligue Contre La Cancer; Air France etc.

A warm thanks to all the hospitals and their staff who have welcomed clown-doctors in their midst. And last but never least, "MERCI" to all the children and their families who have offered us their smiles, laughter and strong moments of shared emotion.

Contents

Clowns & Fools Come Out to Play: A Preface to
the English Language Version   xi

Introduction   1

1.	"Clowns here, are you joking?"	9
2.	Inclownito	11
3.	"You aren't doctors"	13
4.	"Guess what we do'	17
5.	Atmospheres	21
6.	La Mouche and Giraffe go exploring	23
7.	"Ladies and Gentlemen, step right up!"	25
8.	First dose of "Osteo-humorology"	29
9.	"Balmy"	33
10.	Three Little Words	35
11.	Still able to giggle	39
12.	Bobissimo	43
13.	Trust	45
14.	Clouds	49
15.	Wings and Stars	53
16.	Countless Metaphors	57
17.	"Hallo, Miffter Momo!"	61
18.	The Giraffe and the Dragonfly	65
19.	The show must go on	67
20.	"Choose life!"	71
21.	Our small tribe	73
22.	Professor Pewpew levitates	75
23.	Chic, another clown husband!	77
24.	"In like"	81
25.	Cumulus	83
26.	On the high wire	87
27.	I'm Dreaming of a white Christmas	89
28.	Clippity-Clop	91
29.	April Showers for Winter flowers	93
30	Where's the Sanity Claus?	95
31	A Leek in the Oncology Ward	97
32	Let them tears flow	99
33	Silent Night, Holy Night	103
34	Swine Lake	105
35	Tap dancing in a minefield	107
36	Syncopation	109
37	Dr. Josephine and already 70 "guests"	111

38	"I want my clowns right now!"	115
39	A day with Coco-a-Gogo	117
40	Rituals	119
41	"Y'all should entertain in a zoo!"	123
42	Pierrette, alias Dr. Basket	127
43	I'm back	131
44	The gift of life	133
45	Excuses	135
46	"La vie en rose"	139
47	Dr. Dora, Dr. Sam, Dr. Balthazar and Co.	143
48	Crying Wolf with a Duck Call	147
49	Two Beauti-fool Flowers Open	149
50	Back Home with the Clown-Doctors	151
51	National Poetry Week	155
52	Reverse Psychology	157
53	The Art of Observation	161
54	Emotions	163
55	"Something has changed here"	167
56	Signature	169
	Le Rire Medecin Clowns	171
	Code of Ethics: Le Rire Medecin	173

Welcome to a *Probing the Boundaries* Project

Making Sense of: Health, Illness and Disease is an inter-disciplinary and multi-disciplinary research project which aims to explore the processes by which we attempt to create meaning in health, illness and disease. The project examines the models we use to understand our experiences of health and illness (looking particularly at perceptions of the body), and evaluates the diversity of ways in which we creatively struggle to make sense of such experiences and express ourselves across a range of media.

Among the themes explored by the project are:

- the 'significance' of health, illness and disease for individuals and communities
- the concept of the 'well' person; the preoccupation with health; the attitudes of the 'well' to the 'ill'; perceptions of 'impairment' and disability; the challenges posed when confronted by illness and disease; the notion of being 'cured'; chronic illness; terminal illness; attitudes to death
- how we perceive of and conduct ourselves through the experiences of health and illness
- 'models' of the body; the body in pain; biological and medical views of illness; the ambiguous relationship with 'alternative' medicine and therapies; the doctor-patient relationship; the 'clinical gaze'
- the impact of health, illness and disease on biology, economics, government, medicine, politics, social sciences; the potential influences of gender, ethnicity, and class; health care, service providers, and public policy
- the nature and role of 'metaphors' in expressing the experiences of health, illness and disease - for example, illness as 'another country'; the role of narrative and narrative interpretation in making sense of the 'journey' from health through illness, diagnosis, and treatment; the importance of story telling; dealing with chronic and terminal illness; the 'myths' surrounding health, illness and disease
- the relationship between creative work and illness and disease: the work of artists, musicians, poets, writers. Illness and the literary imagination - studies of writers and literature which take health, disability, illness and disease as a central theme

Dr Robert Fisher
Inter-Disciplinary.Net
http://www.inter-disciplinary.net

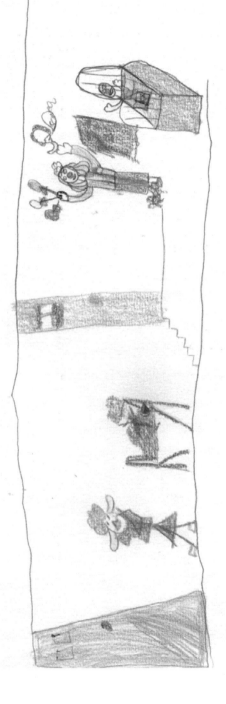

Clowns and Fools Come Out to Play:
A Preface - Of Sorts - to the English Language Version

So why a collaboration between a silly "clown-doctor" and a "fool-professor"?

I discovered Bernie Warren in Manchester, England at a conference I almost didn't go to. Oddly enough, he was the first person I have met who, having never seen or done this work, had an immediate inner sense, wisdom and appreciation of it. While listening to his presentation, I chuckled when he said he was from a Ukrainian Jewish family, I giggled when he said he had dropped out of medical school to become a street performer, I began to get scared when he said that he taught clowning at a University in Canada, that he had done major research on the "fool"; I almost ran in the opposite direction when he described how he had worked with children in hospitals and now taught Qigong to adult cancer patients. Without looking, I had found my writing partner...There are no coincidences.

Until meeting Bernie Warren, I was asked too many times when I was going to write a book about Le Rire Medecin, the French clown-doctor adventure. At least 3 different people have wanted to collaborate, including my ex-shrink, an art school director and a Professor of Endocrinology. Oddly enough, a fellow clown has never asked to play this duet and the prospect of a solo was terrifying.

On First Meeting la Giraffe

I first met Caroline Simonds, aka Dr. Josette Giraffe, on April 13th 1999 at a World Symposium on Culture, Health and the Arts. The symposium was hosted by Peter Senior, a leading catalyst in the development of the concept of "Arts for Health". Peter and I have been friends and colleagues for 20 years and I had been trying unsuccessfully to sit and talk with him all evening. I decided to 'cut my losses' and was in a stairwell with about a dozen others bidding our host good night. At the same Caroline was engaging Peter with her concerns about her next morning's presentation and the fact that she had to introduce Patch Adams. Leaving him to the crowd, Caroline and I walked down the stairs together and started talking.

Our collaboration started slowly, we found out from our journey down the stairs that we shared certain interests. We politely agreed to attend each other's session in the morning. As the conference wore on, we began to realize just how much of our work shared common threads. Even more than that, as discussions about our work progressed, we started to look back at our respective upbringings and trainings to see why we have such similarities in our lives. To cut a long story short, within 2 months of this first meeting we decided to write this book together.

Where to begin..?

When we first began writing we felt we were in a rudderless boat, lost without a compass. We had lots of ideas, pages of scribbled notes, some great starting points but no sense of direction. After writing some interesting pieces, that really had no connection one with the other, we simultaneously came up with a question, "who the hell are we writing for?"

The answer did not come all at once. We spent a lot of time discussing who would want to read our work. We were clear on what we did not want to do. We both wanted to avoid "preaching to the converted" and we neither of us felt comfortable trying to make this an "Academic Text Book" to be read solely by Medical professionals or by students of medicine , nursing or theatre. One day in the course of our discussions Caroline suddenly blurted out, "I'd like my 95 year old neighbour in Quinson, Madame Maubert to be able to read this". Almost spontaneously I replied, "I'd like my 4 year old daughter, Alora to read this when she is 12 (why 12? I'm not sure...). These simple thoughts acted as a beacon, a light by which we guided our vessel of creativity.

We started slowly. As we wrote we tried to 'speak' to several friends and relatives of all ages (4-95) who symbolized for us the people we wanted to reach: young and old; men and women; professionals, trades people and homemakers in cities, towns and villages; for laughter and illness know no boundaries.

Later that same lifetime....

So 4 years ago we began to write this book . Caroline and I spent 2 years of our lives researching and writing together supported by various grants and foundations, The University of Windsor and Le Rire Medecin (our employers) and of course by our families. In 2001 our work was translated from the original English (and greatly enriched) by Marie-France Girod and published in French as "Le Rire Medecin: journal du docteur Girafe".

In the time since the book was first published the work of Le Rire Medecin has gone from strength to strength. The size of the company has grown and we now employ 48 clown-doctors. We continue to see more than 40,000 sick and hospitalised children each year. In addition to the Paris, Nantes and Orleans programs we offer a new satellite program in Marseilles and have added two new programs in Paris: 11 hospitals in all. (For more information see: www.leriremedecin.asso.fr)

The work I (BW) did on this book brought all my previous work together. As a direct result of the work with Caroline and my time spent with the clown-doctors of Le Rire Medecin, I began to develop my own clown-doctor programs. In July 2001 I began *Fools For Health* in Windsor, Ontario. The program has gone from strength to strength and now employs 6 full time clown-doctors who work across the lifespan in local hospitals and healthcare facilities. (for more information see www.foolsforhealth.ca).

Without wishing to sound too immodest. We are very proud of this book. For while it is a book that deals with laughter and sorrow and medical issues, I (BW) believe it is above all what my old friend Professor Richard Courtney would have called "a jolly good read". I look forward to my daughter being old enough to read it. In the meantime, dear reader, please enjoy what follows.

Bernie Warren PhD
Professor, Drama in Education and Community
School of Dramatic Art
University of Windsor
CANADA

Caroline Simonds
Artistic Director
Le Rire Medecin
Paris
FRANCE

November 2003

Dr. Giraffe
(Caroline Simonds)
Le Rire Medecin

Dr. Haven't-A-Clue
(Bernie Warren)
Fools For Health

Introduction

There is nothing like a cold dose of reality to put one's life in perspective. My name is Bernie Warren, a Professor of Dramatic Art at the University of Windsor, Canada. I have worked with sick, disabled and disenfranchised people in schools, senior's homes and hospitals for nearly thirty years. I have trained and worked as a comic actor and taught clowning to university students for nearly 20 years. It's October 1999 and here I am in a Parisian children's hospital, standing outside a locked changing room with two "clown-doctors" from Le Rire Médecin, Caroline Simonds (Dr. Giraffe) and her partner Yann Siprott (Dr. Bob). And to tell the truth, I wonder: why am I here?

Le Rire Medecin is a French company that bring smiles, fantasy and laughter to children's bedsides in paediatric hospitals. Caroline Simonds, an American clown, came to Paris from New York in 1991 to create it after performing for 3 and a half years as a member of "The Big Apple Circus Clown Care Unit", the pioneers of this type of work. Today, Le Rire Medecin employs over thirty professionally trained clown-doctors who are an integral component of the health care process in the hospitals in which they perform. They encounter children twice a week all through the year and see approximately 30,000 hospitalised children per year. They have a code of ethics, engage in continuous training and they are briefed by the staff about the medical needs and progress of each child before they see him. They are not there to simply entertain. They are members of a treatment team, working to improve a child's well-being and quality of life.

I first encountered the work of Caroline earlier this year at the first World Symposium on Culture, Health and the Arts in Manchester, England. As I had already spent over ten years researching the use of humour and laughter in health care, I was immediately fascinated. By the end of the conference, Caroline and I realised that our work shared many common threads and within two months of our first meeting we decided to write this book together.

Clown-doctors of "Le Rire Medecin" are not physicians, they are a special breed of performer! Each has an identifiable and unique personality, trademark and name e.g. Dr. Giraffe (ears, horns and a detachable tail); Dr. Chic (Formal dress shirt, Scottish kilt and a French beret); and, Dr. Coco-a-Gogo (red elf hat and a mini-skirt). In addition to his own costume, each has a personalised and decorated white medical coat. This makes the white coats of the medical staff less scary and at the same time identifies them as part of the medical team.

The clowns often carry a variety of props in their pockets or in their "doctor bags" e.g., slide whistles made from syringes; telephones made from stethoscopes; traditional musical instruments of all kinds;

banana-maracas; pickles that squeak; bubble blowers; finger puppets etc. Essentially any object, medical device or toy that is found in a patient's room can be transformed and used as a theatrical tool. They believe less is more. Finally and most importantly, all the performers wear a red nose, "the smallest mask in the world." It is the glue that holds the clown-doctor's character together.

The clown-doctors of Le Rire Medecin work in pairs called "clown marriages." Usually one performer plays a "white" clown, a rational voice of reason, the orderly decision maker; while the other plays an "auguste", who is fun loving, impulsive and often the "trouble maker." Each partner has his own style, set of skills, comic bits, gestures, music and particular clown vocabulary. Some do not use a spoken language and some use a highly stylised vernacular of vocal sounds and utterances (nonsense words, animal noises, squeaks etc.). As a clown character, they are, or say, something "distinctive", but share certain skills, sensitivities and attributes. They all have the ability to listen actively and fully, communicate through words, music or even through the "inspired" use of silence and to see the "one door" they can open for a child.

Today I am here at Caroline's invitation. This is planned to be the first of several visits to observe the performers at work in different hospitals to try to understand what it means to work as a clown-doctor. I am conscious of how exceptional it is to allow a visitor in at so early a point in the life of this brand new program. I want to help, not hinder my friends. It doesn't help that my French is rusty and I have come here merely to observe. Caroline said to "come 'dressed as a wall'". I feel that in so many ways, nothing has prepared me for this.

In the nurse's locker room, the clowns are stepping out of civilian clothes and putting on their costumes. I'm trying to make myself scarce. Unfortunately Yann (Dr. Bob) is like a wonderfully friendly puppy and every time I try to blend in with the walls he is encouraging me to participate as they warm up.

To enter the haematology ward we have to go through a double set of electronic doors. The kids in here are so sick that every precaution is taken to hold back the outside world. We don't move fast as the 3 of us engage in comic business with the doors. For Dr. Giraffe (Caroline) and Dr. Bob (Yann) this is possibly a mundane procedure, warming up and simply preparing to "Make an Entrance." I tell my drama students that entrances and exits are both the most difficult and the most important things that an actor does.

As we prepare to go through the second set of "airlocks" the clowns start their parade music, so that as they enter the ward, everyone knows they have arrived. I peel off from them and merge with a door so that I may watch as they entertain a few families lingering in the entrance way. Next a little banter with Mimi, the receptionist, and then they pop their noses in to see, first the head nurse and then the head doctor. I straggle about four paces behind, feeling like a Sheik's new wife. I am formally introduced. Already it's getting hard to blend into the woodwork.

Off we go again, a little processional music, a few comic bits as we walk down the hallway. After a few minutes we are at the nurse's station and both clowns go into "noses down" mode as they take notes. There are about ten of us (clowns, nurses, doctors, interns), all in this small space. Everywhere I move I seem to be in the way of one of the nurses.

By the end of a morning of trailing around watching Dr. Bob and Dr. Giraffe this feeling has left me. I've relaxed and have found a rhythm of being present without being obtrusive. This ward is basically a square design, giving the sense of fools walking around the village. Stopping at individual rooms is like visiting different houses. While they are a community brought together by disease and suffering, each household is different. However like fools and travelling minstrels before them, these clown-doctors create a feeling of togetherness and leave the gift of laughter at every stop.

Now we are at the Bone Marrow Transplant Unit (B.M.T.U.), a few rooms situated at the far end of the ward. Already I have witnessed how the clowns have to wash their hands before entering every "household." Here they have their own "sanitised" B.M.T.U. costumes. I don a disposable hospital gown and booties. We all wear masks. This special costume has to be put on with gymnastics as you enter, but before your foot touches the floor on the inside of the unit.

Once inside there are still layers protecting the children. They are on beds behind clear plastic curtains inside sanitised rooms. The clowns are limited; no facial expressions, just eyes. What splendid communication is accomplished. For reasons of hygiene, they use no props, only what is in the room. I'm seeing poetry at work. They are using the child as the third point of the triangle. The child is both audience and player in the improvised dramas and is balancing the creative tensions between the two clowns: the auguste and the white clown. I've already seen the way they integrate others into the work but what I see in this unit leaves me speechless.

On a break, time to reflect. It is amazing to see the virtuosity of these two "clown-doctors." They are maestro's of improvisation. They silently fall in love with a television or lie prostrate on their knees in supplication; they are part of a violent and loud video game or an induced death fantasy. The range is incredible and the choices are subtle. I wish my students could see this.

Often the work is for an audience of one. If there are other people in the room, such as parents, doctors, nurses, cleaners, anybody, they are co-opted by the performers to become a part of the travelling show that just happens to be playing at a "hospital bedside near you". They are geniuses at transforming even the most dour-faced 'maiden aunt' into an apprentice

4

or a full-fledged fool. The "villagers" here are both audience and players sharing the joy of a modern-day equivalent of a 'feast of fools' in a well-equipped, modern hospital.

Yet the events of this day remind me that the clowns are human. The level of suffering and pain that these children live with, silently and not so silently, defies description. The clowns are not always successful, at least not in the sense that most people would judge the work. They do not always bring a smile to the child's face. One girl's screams are heart wrenching. She is about the same age as my daughter Alora. I feel tears forming as I listen. The clowns are unable to help. Whatever is going on in there at this moment is even beyond the reach of these "magicians of the soul." They play some soft tunes and leave. Shortly before they are to finish for the day they re-enter dragging all and sundry in their wake, creating a whirlwind of action. Now, the child laughs, I cry and say a silent thank you for the good health of my own child.

At the end of the day, I know I have witnessed one of those great "change moments" in my life. I have read, written and talked about the power of humour in healing many times before, but this was the first time I had truly felt it.

***

This book tells a story that takes place over a few months in 1999-2000, eight years after Le Rire Medecin was created. Through the eyes of Caroline Simonds, it describes the development of a new program in a paediatric hospital and all the challenges that a clown-doctor is confronted with over and over. Most of the children that are described had been diagnosed with leukaemia and other serious forms of cancer. Some 20 years ago, not many survived these illnesses but nowadays, they can be cured in four out of 5 cases. However, there is still a risk of death. The patients that appear here were hospitalised often and ran this risk. The children doing well medically were in the hospital less often.

This book is a tale of love and humour and of dealing with great traumas and tragedy. It tells of the immense compassion and the amazing resilience of individuals in the most stressful and debilitating of circumstances. It is a small window looking onto what it is to be human with all our strengths and frailties and of how complete strangers can become bonded to one another through laughter and pain.

While all names (except the clown's) and locations are changed, out of respect for confidentiality and medical secrecy, the stories presented here are based upon real case studies from Caroline's own experiences with occasional commentaries from me to put her experiences into perspective. Above all else this book is a celebration and an homage to all the children, their parents and care-givers who have shared their lives with Caroline and her fellow clown-doctors over the past years.

Bernie Warren Ph.D.
Professor, School of Dramatic Art
University of Windsor
Canada   February 2001

A child with a life-threatening condition is like an exotic flower. When we cut that flower, we can keep it alive in water. Either it grows strong roots and survives the injury to its stem or it will wilt and die. Whatever happens, we enjoy the beauty of this flower. We must honour its life, the joy it gives us. The exquisite loveliness of those fragile moments together. I walk into a garden fluttering with truth.

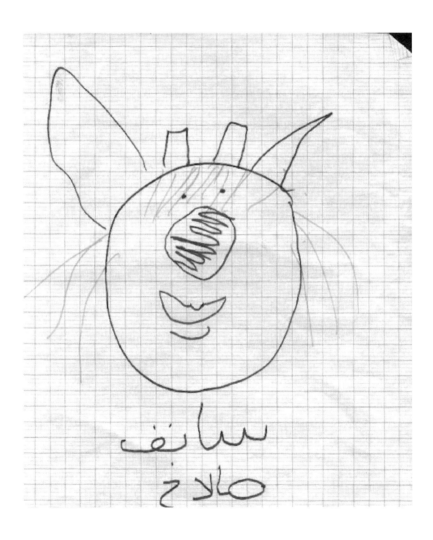

1.

"Clowns *here*, are you joking?"

"We don't need clowns here, we have free shows at Christmas and volunteers to do arts and crafts with the kids all year round." It has taken me six months to get my foot in the door. After letters and calls the Professor has accorded me 15 minutes of his day; this is all he can give me. I know he is a busy man with a mountain of responsibilities. Here I am in his office, surrounded by diplomas and medical books. Maybe I should just go home.

My heart is racing as I explain that I have been working regularly in paediatric hospitals as a clown-doctor since 1988 in the U.S.A.; (will I ever get in all the information that I want him to hear?) that my company has been working in France for the last eight years, even in other sections of this hospital and that the evaluations with numerous health care teams have been positive. Dozens of hospitals want Le Rire Medecin. Many parents write to request us, hundreds of clowns send their resumes. We are almost treated like a "public service."

I explain that we are eager to develop a program "chez-lui" because of the fine reputation his staff has created; a welcoming atmosphere for children with leukaemia. Plus the research they do here is outstanding. We would like to work with them as part of a global approach to hospital care. We do not want to distract the children from their illness but rather to help them cope with hospitalisation.

The professor sits behind his mahogany desk asking me a series of candid questions. "Why are you drawn to children with life-threatening diseases? What is your background? Do the clowns do shows in the playroom or the waiting room, how about the individual rooms? What prepares them for working in a hospital? Do you think that laughter is therapeutic? Why do you pay performers to do this work when you can get volunteers?" I keep talking as quickly as possible, knowing that at any moment that he might have to leave and pray that my answers are convincing. This man sparkles with intelligence as he listens.

He warns me that we could never start without the approval of the parent's association (who aren't particularly fond of clowns), the head nurse (who isn't particularly fond of clowns) and his entire staff (who, I hope, adore clowns). He adds that he does not have a red cent in his piggy bank to invest in this program. I let him know that we have been offered funding for a 3 year project in his ward. Then ask him if his team is willing to welcome and work with professional artists, including conducting semi-annual evaluations as well as developing various research projects together. We are not coming in to fill dysfunctional voids. I realise that I am beginning to like this dignified man.

When the Professor finally stands up, I automatically look at my watch and see that this fifteen minute discussion has turned into two hours. Suddenly he seems impatient and before I can thank him for his time, he asks: "By the way, I want you to meet my staff soon and if they give the "go-ahead" when will our clown-doctor program start?" I cannot believe my ears. I dash out before he can change his mind. Wait till they hear clown noise.

2.

Inclownito

Inclownito or undercover clown is a code that clowns use when they are "disguised" as ordinary people in everyday clothing! On the other hand, when I put on my clown-make up, I feel as if I am washing away the human.

This is my first (inclownito) visit to observe the ward. I should say, our first visit. La Giraffe (my "nom de scene") is not alone in the lion's den. I am with Nadine, alias, La Mouche, my co-conspirator and clown partner. We get along fabulously, are complementary in our artistic skills and harmonious in the auguste - white clown dynamic. Nadine is a natural communicator, with tolerance for the range in personalities that can be encountered within a hospital staff. I can count on her through thick and thin; and rely on her to do half the seduction job that is required at first with a new medical team. When you're in with the nurses, you're in a club of sisters! So, we enter into our clown marriage for better or for worse.

On our first stroll into the haematology unit, I notice that it is four-sided with bizarre corners like a village square. The B.M.T.U. is situated at the far end. The children's rooms are all along the window-sides as well as two in each corner. The silence is ominous. I suppress my urge to sing and make NOISE. In the centre are small rooms for the doctors to bury their noses in folders, study x-rays, write up reports, and another one for the nurses to concoct potions. Because of the bay windows, everyone looks like human tadpoles in giant aquariums. I fight an urge to tell tacky fish jokes. I tell one anyway. A nurse attempts a half-inch smile. I better sit on my tongue, Nadine is giving me one of her dark-eyed looks. The kids have rooms on all four window sides with itty-bitty portals looking onto the corridors. There are a few huge photos showing tropical island views with smiling kids (probably former patients) in swim suits or on sail boats.

There is an odour of "lull." It feels like everyone is suspended by invisible silk threads waiting for an arrival or an interruption. I see brown eyes peering out from behind a door. A solitary plump boy, maybe 5 years old and a shiny bald head, promenades his I.V. pole, almost like one would walk a dog around and around the right angled halls. It's so quiet. It reminds me of the old people in remote villages eternally waiting on their stone benches. My mind needs to wander: Maybe a ravishing blonde bombshell will waltz in? Will it snow, right here in these hallways? Maybe there will be spice cake for dinner. I want to fly away, escape while I still can. What are we getting ourselves into? This place is craving for chaos, the unexpected. It's hard to be a filly at the starting gate, waiting for the gun to go off.

3.

"You aren't doctors"

A week later, since Nadine is not available, I invite Guy, Dr. Gustave (who has worked with L.R.M. for 5 years) to help me present the project to members of the staff. On the day before the powwow, Guy and I have lunch to discuss how to "sell our clown soup." We both have serious stage fright and are determined to use it to fuel our arguments and strategies. We feel condemned to succeed.

The next day, 20 poker-faced nurses, interns and doctors wait in a windowless room for our "dog and pony" show. The Professor is not there so as not to influence his team. Guy and I partner inclownito, balancing each other's phrases with anecdotes and humour. In case of an emergency, Guy has concealed some of the tools of our trade in his briefcase: a red nose, some bubbles and a squeaker. Squeakers are small noisemakers that clowns can conceal in their palm to create the illusion of a funny sound coming from the tip of a nose or a belly button. We show a dozen slides that illustrate how we will work in their ward. A day in the life of a clown-doctor.

At first we are met with silence and aloof glances. This is not trial by fire, it is trial by ice. I am worried. Slowly some questions and concerns are being voiced. The tone is warming up. One nurse asks: "Why do you call yourselves clown-doctors when you are not trained physicians?" Guy catches that hard ball and responds eloquently. This is a turning point but the actual break-through comes when I show a slide of a nurse in an intensive care unit crouching next to an adolescent patient who is "sprouting wings." This is a code that my American partner Kim, Dr. Loon and I developed when we started performing regularly at a children's hospital in the Bronx. It means that a patient is reaching the last part of his life. He might cease to live at any moment, but he is not dying. He is growing feathers, sprouting wings and will soon fly away. In the slide, two male clowns are at the bedside, playing a delicate serenade.

Few people in a hospital are able to pronounce the word, death. Nurses, doctors and others, each have their codes for the word. Over the years, I have heard things that seem either too bland or too cruel for the delicacy of announcing a child's death: "She's gone to a better place", or "He's now on the left bank", gone, vanished, erased.

When I was a clown-doctor in the Bronx, the first losses were the worst and hit like napalm in my soul. I had no idea how to position myself. Who was I to my patients and who were they to me? Especially when they died on me (with or without warning), their parents, their care givers. Could anyone go back to the hospital after experiencing such mourning and grief? It felt scandalous, I wasn't even "family or friend", yet I had become attached. This was confusing. The bonds to the children were so powerful that when they left the earth, I lost all clarity as to my role.

So in our pain, I created the infamous "cherub code" to help cope with the flight of life and the blitz of departure for our young patients. At the time this felt taboo and naughty, but it seemed to help us get through some hard times. When I remembered my wings as a street performer, the images materialised. Starting timidly one day, I whispered to my partner: "I see feathers growing on that little one. Maybe he is sprouting wings." Over the years we imagined other "codes": "Voyage to the shooting stars, she's on the runway, ready for take off, Blast Off!" Then nicknames for children who had already died: "Angel Brigade, Flock of Birds, King of the Stratosphere."

So why is talking about death such a taboo? In the beginning, I often felt incoherent and overwhelmed, it was so difficult to put the right words onto such powerful feelings. Believe me, this still occurs. How to mourn a child's relapse, deal with finding another amputated, disfigured by illness, paralysed, in a coma or the unexpected loss of a little pal? How are we to separate the professional from the private so that we can last a long time as hospital clowns without unnecessary burnout and loss of sensitivity? After all, a clown must stay in a state of wonder, naiveté. Clown-doctors need poetic humour to balance both tragedy and hilarity on their red noses.

Back in the meeting a second question fires out: "Do you really think it is appropriate for two clowns to intrude on a patient's end-of-life moments? Does the family really accept your presence?" So, how are we to answer? Is there a "perfect" response? Guy and I spontaneously leave 30 seconds of silence before gently describing our past years of experience with the "angel brigade." The dozens of serenades, unexpected giggle-fits with grandparents, how we can take sisters and brothers as our assistants while parents hover over a bed in a darkened room.

The key moment of change comes when we acknowledge their work in this hospital with children who are in danger of dying. We say how gargantuan and heart-breaking it is for them on a daily basis. There is a physical shift in the room's energy, something has released and opened. Guy and I look at each other and know, they aren't just letting us in a window, they are letting us in the front door! The dialogue goes on way over the planned hour.

Before leaving the hospital, we distribute our code of ethics and leave a dozen or so brochures for nurses and doctors who missed the meeting. There is one last question: "So when do y'all start?" (Breathe, Caroline. Breathe, Guy). I answer: "What about Monday?" We hear a few soft cheer! And I run to tell the Professor.

When an actor arrives at a hospital, he is a human being who must transform into a clown-doctor. Each has his ways of changing. For a few the change starts as soon as he enters the hospital building. Simply sitting alone drinking coffee begins the process and little by little the clown persona starts to appear.

For most it is far more individual and complex. Many performers spend long periods of contemplative preparation, moving step by step towards the development of their clown-doctor persona. For some of the L.R.M. performers their clown-doctor is a stylised version of himself. They find elements of their own lives and use these as catalysts for their character.

Many have a specific technique, action or costume piece that makes it possible for them to transform into their clown. Examples include putting on their Rire Medecin white coat, makeup or red nose (often the first or the last piece of costume to be put on); singing a particular song or even simply finding a voice or an accent peculiar to their character. For others, it is only when they engage in the first playful interactions with their partner that they truly feel "in clown." Finally, for a few L.R.M. performers, they need to take a moment to take in the patients and to see how the public is transformed by their character.

However, the clown is not the only one who must change. He needs to transform the hospital space from a place of seriousness to a fun filled village square where anything can happen. To do this they must metamorphose their audience: patients, their families and any of the hospital staff. No one is exempt: kings and commoners; doctors and orderlies; duchesses and serving maids; nurses and, volunteers. It is a delicate process because each "villager" must accept that they are on the clown-doctor's dance card. In so doing, start to play an active part in their journey to an improved quality of life.

4.

"Guess what we do?"

I meet Nadine at 9 A.M. and our first act of the day is to have coffee on the ground floor cafeteria. As usual, Nad inhales her brew boiling hot while I blow and sip on mine for the next 10 minutes. The place is full of smoke, loud and unfriendly. We decide that we will not enjoy eating lunch here. Ever.

For the second act of the day, after a painless elevator ride to the 5th floor, we introduce ourselves to the medical secretaries. The best way to maintain a great relationship with any hospital staff is to honour the secretaries. They are the heartbeat of the unit and most information filters down from them. Then we go to shake hands with the Professor and meet a few of his colleagues. They look wary but remain proper. Then on to greeting the head nurse, the queen of the mountain. In the hallways we perceive three volunteers, elegant despite their pink uniforms. Clowns call them, the "Chanel No. 5 and Ruby Brigade." Also three or four teachers scampering into rooms laden with book bags. They look on beyond serious. I smell attitude.

There are no patients hanging out in the hallways, but we run into a 13 year old "guest", (a more civilised term for a haematology patient) who's waiting for a chemo treatment. We recognise her dad and remember that we had known her older brother, treated years before in the oncology ward of this same hospital. (Oh my god, two kids in the same family with cancer). We play an undercover clown game with her. Guess what profession we do? "Physiotherapists?" "No", "Artists?" "Yes." "Clowns?" It doesn't take her long. She has been humouring us. All the while in just the next room with at least five nurses around him, a young child squeals bloody murder for 10 solid minutes. It's unbearable. The kid's mom cries softly in a corner near us, while her little one is being pierced by god knows what instrument. Why isn't she in the room with her child? The realisation that we are helpless in the inclownito state upsets me. This is too frustrating. My clown instincts are howling to play soft music, at least for the mom, to soothe her shattered nerves. Probably our own too. There is work to be done with the nurses as well as the screamer. Everyone looks frazzled.

Then we have several mini-meetings. The first is with a doctor who gives us the following information that compliment what the Professor had said; "80% of our patients can be cured." (How about the ones I'll see here?) "Brain tumours are a catastrophe, so are neuroblastomas, we treat leukaemia. Not so many deaths here like in oncology." Nadine looks relieved. Her two years in oncology was like a war. "The first hospitalisation is usually a medical emergency. The illness is acute. Every new patient is greeted by a doctor, a nurse and Mimi, the medical secretary at the front desk." I ask who makes the first pronouncement about a diagnosis to a child and his parents. She explains that "the doctor who announces the illness to them will follow his case, including all treatments and protocols, right to remission, cure, an eventual relapse or death. The kids experience less pain here than in the oncology ward." Physical pain? Psychic pain? We'll see.

"The beginning of a treatment is intense and lasts about 5 weeks. The child will have an I.V. pole, that holds the bags of medication, a few invasive procedures: Myelograms (myelos), performed in the sternum or the iliac (near the hip) and Lumbar Punctures (L.P.). In the first few days he will go under anaesthesia, to the operating room for a broviac1 to be placed in his chest." This whole procedure seems so horrendous to me at first that the only way I can cope is to invent a softer term, a new code. So I look at Nadine and say: "Sounds like a 'Full Monty' to me". It's an English term for getting a three course breakfast or "the works" (in French: "la totale")! Nad winks back but the doctoress keeps going with her lesson, unperturbed.

"In the first few days of hospitalisation the average kid sees almost 30 new faces (doctors, nurses, lab technicians, etc.). A door can open and close 60 times a day. The children here are isolated to protect them from infection. This is due to a condition called aphasia, where their white blood cell count is low thus they are immune-deficient and subject to infections and frequent fevers. The first chemotherapy treatment or chemo is usually well tolerated with little vomiting, by the third week, after the second chemo, the kids loose their hair, have mouth sores and experience more fatigue." She stops for a second waiting for my commentary. What can I say? Nadine is even quieter. "There is a residence near by for parents to sleep if they cannot spend the night in the room. During the isolation periods, everyone that enters the room, parents included, must wear a mask and wash their hands. Sisters and brothers under the age of 15 may not visit. All visits are limited to two people a day besides a primary parent. A patient is considered to be cured after three years of treatment." Is that all?

Now all we have to do is digest all this information but there's no time for we have a meeting with the psychologist. He adds the following: "Because the kids are mostly in aphasia, all the rooms are for single patients and there is a bed for one parent. This is beneficial for younger children but maybe problematic for adolescents, who need more autonomy and privacy." If I were 17 and had my mom sleeping in my room for 5 weeks, I would want to kill her. "In both cases, the children become heavily bonded to the parent who "sleeps in." It is not easy for the parent who may suffer from isolation and lack of contact with his or her partner and home life." Bonjour le stress. What about a weekly massage?

"There are usually 3-5 adolescents hospitalised at a time and there are no activities for them except the school teachers, T.V., sometimes a computer and a small selection of videos." Hey what about telephones? "The transformation of their body preoccupies them."

"After a Bone Marrow Transplant (B.M.T.), the children's bodies change. They puff up from the cortisone treatments. Their diets are restricted." No sugar, no candy, to comfort them.

Finally we meet Mimi, who works all week at the front desk. She welcomes the patients and their families for hospitalisations as well as for the day hospital, answers a myriad of questions for everyone (from check-in and check-out procedures, the time the Professor makes his rounds, to where to buy deodorant in the neighbourhood), and directs traffic, working with the head nurse to co-ordinate and schedule all appointments for patients e.g., x-ray, scanner, physiotherapist, biopsies, surgery). I can feel that Mimi will always be able to give us a reality check and a "weather report"! This is another code word for getting the "low down" on the general ambience in the ward. "Stormy weather" might mean that there are some delicate patients around today. "Blue skies" may mean that there is nothing abnormal happening for the moment. Beware of lightning? Mimi is the pulse of all activity, like the village "grocer" or the matchmaker or the rabbi.

What a day. By late afternoon our brains are buzzing and we are ready to cut out and cool down. We need to shake a tail-feather and I had just received an invitation to a hot cocktail party on the other end of town. So, that evening, after a day of an overwhelming amount of information, Nadine and I find ourselves nose to nose with the head nurse at the bar of the event. She is even more surprised than us. It's pure serendipity. Two glasses of champagne and some rocking and rolling later, our trio is bonded. Now "Madame" likes clowns. Me and la Nad, anyway. Make way for the red nose transplant team.

Clown-doctors do not make a medical diagnosis or write a case history, rather they create their own prescription, one that does not focus on the patient's limitations but instead on those parts of the individual that are healthy. They help parents and the rest of the medical team realise that a patient is not simply his illness. In doing this, parents and the medical team are all able to see beyond the disease and enable patients to take responsibility for something as simple as deciding whether or not to laugh. In this way clown-doctors give everyone a gift of sight.

However, because the clown-doctors can work outside the constraints of hospital policies and procedure they can do what is needed, not simply what is allowed. Sometimes this does not endear them to other professionals and occasionally this causes animosity amongst other team members. But it is important to remember that it's not a competition. hey are colleagues who complement one another.

5.

Atmospheres

A few days later, ready for another day of observations, Nad and I meet in the cafeteria and go up to the 5th trying not to get lost in the labyrinth of hallways. Are all hospitals alike? First they mess with your sense of direction and then they mess with your body.

Setting up the dressing room is essential for performers. In this ritual, we paste up a few pictures, a tacky circus poster, clean dust from the top of our lockers, and learn the codes for our padlocks. This is the smallest space that I have ever had to prepare in, no chair and no table. We share it with all the nurses. It will be a challenge for two six-foot tall women with long limbs to get costumed without hitting each other in the face.

Then it's coffee and a schmooze (Yiddish for small talk) with the head nurse, now nicknamed, The Queen Bee, (in French, "la Rein Mere)".

Coining nicknames and inventing clown codes help us see staff differently and transform the conventional into the creative. We use nicknames and abbreviations copiously. We use them for patients, but also for the medical staff and naming illnesses. It is a form of affectionate irreverence which allows the doctors and nurses to gently float down from their "medical pedestal", to be treated as real human beings not "clinical-automatons." This affectionate irreverence is one of the clown-doctor's tools for making a positive yet destabilising connection with staff, thus creating a long lasting bond. One that can be built upon with hilarious or tender variations. Because nothing had ever resembled our special relationship with a hospital team, a process had to be invented in order to justify our playful behaviour towards each other.

The nun in oncology has been christened "little sista" by most of our clowns; we usually greet the woman at the head of the cleaning crew by a "Hello Captainette!" In the oncology ward, the lady doctor who sticks kids for the L.P.s has been named "Mizzzzzz Porcupine" and the nurse who runs blood tests in the day clinic has been baptised: "Madame Mosquito."

The day flies by quickly this time. We are beginning to feel more at home. We meet with some of the teachers and they seem slightly territorial. So who does a patient belong to besides himself! Learning to use the washing machine is another important element so that our costumes for the B.M.T.U. may be cleaned and sterilised in house. We eat our first meal in the nurse's lunchroom. Make sure to bring your own salad dressing and put your name on it. Lots to remember.

The rest of the day is consumed with collecting "two minute samples" of hospital sounds, sights and smells.

As for sounds: A television is blaring; slippers padding towards me; "Victor, are you pretending?"; mother scolding a child; ten different voices; wheels squeaking; Two nurses humming; some screaming; water rushing out of a faucet; radio muzak; hollow boxes shuffling; squeak-squeak of rubber soles; a door opens; (sweet toned female voice)"go.........ooops, pardon!...that's good"; a door slams shut; " Now there..." (singsong and feminine); cocktail of hubbub and brouhaha; high heeled shoes go tic tic tac; bare feet squeaking in high heeled sandal shoes; tapping on a table; drrrrrring, "telephone" the beep, beep, beep of a medical pump.

As for smells: dry radiator heat; the lipstick on my upper lip; a hodgepodge of foods heating up (mashed potatoes and mystery chicken); cleaning products; my own perfume, vetivier; an antiseptic (chlorine?).

Finally, what we see: The floor is an orange-ca ca mystery; nurses uniforms are almond-paste pink; walls are sepia and "Isabella" or dirty white; (Princess Isabella waited for 20 years for her true love to reappear never taking off her "white" wedding dress); ceilings a wet rust; goose poop green chairs. Through the window I see a "Paris grey" wall with luminous emerald ivy; multicoloured exotic island beach photos and children's drawings; fire engine-red alarms on walls and; a crib in the hall has pale egg yoke and light blue sheets.

This listening, looking and smelling tradition emerged while training a group of performers in Geneva after the nurses had complained that they were "too loud." I was curious to understand the clown noise in its daily context because we perceive sound differently depending upon what we are accustomed to hearing, seeing or smelling. It is astounding how even the unbearable racket of a jackhammer can go unnoticed in a hospital if it has been assimilated as a part of the scenery.

6.

La Mouche and Giraffe go exploring

Nadine and I take another full day to rehearse musical repertoire and plan theatrical strategy for our first clown performances in the haematology unit. We shop for cloth to be made into special silly gowns and berets for us to wear in the B.M.T.U. We find some tacky 50's polka-dotted and flowered cottons that can be washed at 90 degrees centigrade. We are going to look so stupid. My neighbourhood seamstress promises them for Monday morning.

We decide to introduce ourselves as twin tourists; La Mouche: "Hi, we're sisters..." and Dr. Giraffe: "We don't have the same father"... La Mouche: "... and we don't have the same mother...". We will present ourselves as voyagers who have landed onto an exotic island from a distant clown planet and we need to scrutinize, decode and sample the local vegetation, animal life, food and customs so as to "report home."

In addition to the flute, Giraffe will carry the Polaroid camera and La Mouche will have a picnic basket containing our "gear": binoculars, a plastic magnifying glass, all sorts of maps and 3 dozen red foam noses, which we'll need to "transplant" onto nurses, a few ridiculous hats to dress up the "guests", guide books, sun glasses, a flute, percussion instruments in the shape of pickles and eggs, a dozen postcards that show off "our clown" tribe, Lili and Lola, twin mouse puppets (just in case we meet up with a frightened two-year-old), two bottles of bubble blow (the clown's Swiss army knife), mini note pads, to record the list of places we have seen and people we have met, a pack of high quality coffee and a bar of dark chocolate, to leave in the nurses station and our lunch. Less is more?

It would not be an exaggeration to say that 50% of a clown doctor's day is spent playing music or singing. I have been a musician since the age of eight when I "borrowed" a flute from my mother's lingerie drawer and insisted on taking lessons from a neighbourhood jazz bass player. To find the first clowns for Le Rire Medecin about 50 different performers were interviewed. After meeting a few fabulous musicians with comic possibilities, I concluded that the company would be far better off with fine clowns who had minimal musical skills and that we could develop musical training workshops for the performers. When I hire someone, they must promise to develop their musicality. While it is not essential to become a virtuoso, it is important to master good timing and have a good ear for improvisations. All 31 performers in L.R.M. sing and play an instrument, ranging from the slide whistle and the kazoo to the ukulele and the accordion. Music can speak to the most unreachable people: kids in comas, anguished parents, harassed nurses.

Nadine has a deep voice, almost a baritone. We prepare a dozen musical numbers ranging from romantic ballads (Stormy Weather, Over the Rainbow), to 'faux-rap' plus a few classical pieces: a Mozart vocal duet (Les Nocturnes) and a Bach flute solo accompanied by the pickle-maracas. We have also invented our theme song: "We are the garbage can sisters and we cannot find our misters.. la la la do si do" ad musicum. This might get us on stage, oops, I mean into the first room.

7.

"Ladies and Gentlemen, step right up!"

It's our first full day on the ward. Show time, show time! Ladies and gentlemen, step right up! Greetings this morning are gentle and no one seems shocked to see us arrive inclownito. As we walk through the automatic doors, "Bonjour les clowns!" shouted by the head nurse comes as a blessing. It takes one hour to get our first nurses report familiarising us with all the patients. Our relationship with the staff "out of clown" costume is always calmer and makes it is easier to discuss difficult situations. We are not tempted to exaggerate our facial or verbal expressions keeping things as professional as possible. Besides, the nurse sees a colleague facing her, not a clown with her nose pulled off. This way, she doesn't expect to be entertained. That comes later!

The atmosphere in the nurse's station is concentrated yet almost frenetic. The door opens and closes a million times. Medical folders are on every surface and there is a hi-tech workstation for concocting potions. We get reports from 4 different people. I am used to one or two interlocutors at most. We take our time and begin injecting droplets of humour to "set the tone". We are stunned by the number of times the patients are described as depressed. Are the nurses crying for us to help them or are they just telling us how much the children need something else? Otherwise we are getting just the right amount of information about each "guest." We are encouraged to see one or two patients that "really" need us! We plan to see everyone.

Back in the locker room, we are both nervous. We know that real miracles take time, that what we were about to do was not going to be "spectacular." Once in costume and "warmed up", Nadine and I take two symbolic minutes of deep breaths and parade into the hallways with a low key tune, Dr. Giraffe (yours truly) playing that medieval rock favourite, "Green sleeves" with La Mouche, shaking a pickle-maracas. Sound! Cameras! Action! The fools have entered the village. We make our way around the square and change directions a few times, pausing once in a while to enter a patient's room, photograph a native nurse or local doctor. Thank God there is not a crowd following us to see if we "make the kids laugh", a clown's worst nightmare. That happened once. We attempt our first "red nose transplant" on a smiling student nurse. This classic clown-doctor procedure consists of placing a red nose onto a child's or nurse's face.

We continue discovering each nook and cranny of the ward with wonder. There is nothing to prove. We are in a friendly jungle. Staying "in the moment" is what really counts and not doing too much. Gotta be here and now. Leave 'em hungry.

I see our Code of Ethics taped onto the wall in the nurse's station. Now that's a first! I believe this team has taken us seriously. We are meticulous about washing our hands and donning surgical masks whenever required. It's imperative to demonstrate perfect hygiene habits in front of the nurses so that they will trust us. We take them seriously, too.

Thanks to Mimi, the weather lady who sits on the throne of the "welcome wagon", our postcards (that show all the L.R.M. clown's portraits) are in a place where parents and children can take them. She says: "There's not a cloud in the sky today."

Our first hurdle: there are four patients under the age of four who are more or less frightened by us. (Ben, Walter...) Either they keep their distance, refuse to look at us or burst into tears. One wailed. From experience we know how to put space between us and them. After all, they are small children hospitalised with leukaemia. When you think about it, there are good reasons for their apprehensions.

We are tall and we are clowns so it is not surprising that they are frightened by big ladies wearing theatrical make up, colourful costumes and red noses. Being frightened of strangers is normal behaviour for children this age. After the initial trauma of hospitalisation, where they encounter over two dozen new people in the first 2 days, we represent two more faces that they are not ready to "trust." Afterwards, when the isolation period starts, they only see two visitors a day, including one or both parents, plus their nurses. So their world begins to shrink.

We go slowly for time is our guardian angel. After all, these kidlettes stay for an average of three to five weeks at a time. It would be a mistake to go for "successful" or cheap results too quickly. I do know recipes (bubbles, soft lullabies) but using them could create deeper mistrust in these kids. We know we have the luxury of time to develop a process. Nurses are often surprised when a toddler who is receptive with them is frightened by the clowns. We must have patience with them as well.

There is such isolation here. The rooms are separate spaces that function as lonely islands, floating in a timeless medicalised sea where only meals mark the passage of hours. The routines are predictable and boring. The television is on most of the day. The lack of physical freedom, complicated by tall I.V. poles, frequent changes of medication and fever seems to affect the creativity of these small children. Some parents make heroic efforts to maintain play with their kids. Four to five weeks later, when a child may leave his room, they are often shy, fearful and sometimes terrified of the outside world. The room has become a womb/cocoon that has kept them safe. The price to pay is a regression in trust and fear of open spaces.

The experience of chronic pain in the beginning of the illness as well as during the months of treatment is traumatic and each new person who enters the room may or may not become a source of new suffering: a lumbar puncture, a blood test, any examination. Kids spend too much time in a hospital anticipating what might happen to them next.

The emotional intensity of the illness, leukaemia, and the way it was announced to the family affects children who always pick up on this and worry about their parents' well being. Most children only want their parents to be happy. They can easily see a change in the eyes of everyone that comes to visit and become experts at reading facial expressions. People do not look at them the same way anymore and they hate that.

We try to meet Louie who is described by the nurses as a handsome seven-year-old boy with a high I.Q. and a computer obsession. They add that he was revolted by everything in the beginning of his treatment but is adapting quickly and that his parents are quite supportive. Empty room. Mr. Louie is out for a lab test. That computer obsession has got me curious.

In the next room is 6 year old Rosa who has recently relapsed. The nurses describe her as "the anxious type with unpredictable mood swings. She comes from a large family, Mom, is a mess but Dad is cool and 'on the case'. So, when she is with her mom, she is a 'good' girl but when she is with her dad, she is a 'naughty girl'". I like that part already, but won't tell the nurses. They will do a Bone Marrow Transplant (B.M.T.) on her soon to save her life.
On the bed, a strange munchkin is inspecting the ceiling. Her exhausted looking Mom is staring at the blank wall and takes no notice of us. We need 3 tries to hook our fish with a clown number that will pull her focus away from the light bulb. Then spontaneously, Rosa "speaks" in a strange tin voice through her toy gremlin making all kinds of bizarre gurgling, squeaks and squawks. Is it the Twilight Zone or is this kid slowly losing her marbles?

Then we meet Ophelia who is 9 years old, an only child. She too has relapsed after four years of remission. Her mom is home, paralysed in a wheelchair after a car accident many years ago. We are told that "dad is loving, visits often and that Granny is a worry-wart." We are to stay "out of her way".

We first see Ophelia, in soft buttercup flannels sitting cross-legged on a bed populated with furry stuffed tiggers, bears and a ladybug. A pile of tapes are on the bed table. Looks like a selection of music for an adult. Since she has that "I am overwhelmed" glaze in her doe brown eyes, La Mouche and I sneak right into an upbeat, cha-cha-cha. Ophelia mashes and kneads her ladybug to the rhythm, listening with Bambi ears. Granny is out for a smoke, so we don't have to deal with her yet. At the end of our song, the ladybug suddenly disappears into a zipped pocket (for P.J.'s) in Tiggers bum! Nice! With great tact, she shows us what she can do. This kid has true play potential.

28

Further down the hallway is Jasmin from Morocco who is 11 years old and has not left her room in three months. I can't believe it! Dad died recently and mom has left 7 children back home in the care of relatives. The nurses say that "Jasmin doesn't speak French and she lets her mom systematically answer for her but understands everything. They weep often and are despondent."

Nad and I see the four eyes of Scherezade peering out the door window. I've seen those eyes before. Take a risk Giraffe. Go! Jump into the conscious! I burst into a shrill interminable "yoo yoo yoo yoo yoooooooo." In Middle Eastern countries, a "yoo yoo" is a shrill vocal trill used uniquely by women to express grief or celebration. Then upon hearing our vocalisations, the two white toothed smiles, we never thought we'd see, light up the room! After quickly washing our hands and donning a mask, La Mouche enters, undulating and gyrating while I stay at the doorway playing my best Arab-like tunes on the flute. Mother and daughter, joined by an aunt start giggling, clapping in rhythm as we are transported to some intimate female quarters lost in another world, another time zone. I see a curious nurse lingering in the hallway. A crowd of one.

By the end of the day there are two ten year old girls, Priscilla, from the Paris projects and Annie, from the island of Martinique, both wearing clown hats and red noses, and trailing after us everywhere we go. Our first "assistants"! They have stayed in costume all day, even during medical procedures and that seems to have "amused" one and all. As we leave the ward late in the afternoon, we see the two hairless, micro-clownettes thronging at the front desk next to Mimi, answering phones, writing fake "reports" and offering bonbons to anyone passing by. So what is left behind when clowns go home? Two red noses, a yoo yoo, a few sparkling eyes and a giggle?

A clown-doctor is influenced by the rules of theatre but luckily this can occur anywhere. A room needs no special attributes, for it is the simple action of crossing an empty space with others watching which may transform any room into a stage.

The first step is to transform the hospital ward or bedside, a very real and sometimes scary somewhere, into a magical space where anything may happen. To do this, he must enchant his audience and establish a rapport that enables them to forget their surroundings and everyday lives, and allow fantasy and imagination to take over.

It is not enough to convert the room into a theatrical space for it must also be a "safe space". Laughter is the clown-doctor's secret weapon and it is this shared merriment that helps create this safe space. In so doing, they encourage the audience within the hospital room to come together in a shared bond celebrating life!

8.

First dose of "Osteo-humorology"

    3 days later as the two of us waltz up to the welcome wagon area to get our second weather report, I see wide grins on a few nurse's faces but can feel that some are still cautious and reserved. Besides the morning report on the patients, they don't look or talk to us as real people (or colleagues) yet. We are taken aside by two young interns who are leaving after a 6 month stint, making room for two more to take their place. They say that they "can't wait to get away from this tragedy-unit. Can't stand all the death and despair." Nadine gives me one of her famous dark looks. Hadn't we heard just a few days before that there were few deaths in this unit? She was hoping that we would not go through all the mourning that she had experienced in oncology and this intern was bursting her bubble. One of the doctors, a sensitive sweetie, walks by to hang out with little Annie in her room. He might need "clown care" once in a while, for those black eyes tell the story of many a heartache.
    We visit Rosa for the second time. Her dad, a fellow giraffe (6 foot 5"/ 1 m 92), is thrilled to tango with La Mouche as "mademoiselle" observes. Her B.M.T. has started today and smells like an artichoke boiling. In the meantime, Dad performs his movie director act, carefully taking videos of the whole procedure. The dark ruby-coloured marrow, contained in a plastic bag hanging from an I.V. pole slowly drips into Rosa's passive body; The nurse comes in every few minutes to check; Rosa has a baby doll face with eyes that don't miss a detail. There is a chewed up stuffed monkey named Booboo withered on the bed. We go fishing for the right move. BINGO! At La Mouche's insistence, Rosa starts to abuse the toy extravagantly. The torture ritual resembles a spooky scene from a "B" war movie. We cheer with each punch and twist and it is good to see that Rosa is moving and almost glowing! We begin to see the possibilities for interaction. All of this "on camera", of course.
    We steer clear of most of the wee ones so as not to frighten them, but one 2 year old, Walter yelps just when catching a glimpse of us. I leave a homeopathic red nose and a clown family postcard with his dad.
    We make a couple of attempts to see Louie who is either with his granny (she wants nothing to do with clowns), or with a school teacher who wants even less to do with clowns. We get the impression they don't like to share this "guest".
    Annie follows us all afternoon. The nurses report that she had tried to sleep with her red nose on. Since we learn that her mom loves to sing wild Caribbean calypsos, we create a conga line but nobody else joins, it's all too new for the moment. Before trotting off to other rooms Annie asks why my name is Giraffe. Clowns must use their natural flaws

and limitations to the hilt. Being tall, maladroit and overly thin are just a few of my attributes. As a child I had been called many names: Miss Asparagus; Bony Maroni; Skinny Minney and, Giraffe! I didn't have to look far to find a character that spoke to me. Annie scratches my over-sized yellow ears as if to approve of my choice.

Late afternoon, a nurse comes running in our direction saying that Jasmin has just endured a Lumbar Puncture (L.P.) and is a mess. Could we help by cheering her up? Bow wow, I feel like the town's St. Bernard. Sometimes these requests take months in other wards or hospitals. Are we going too quickly? So, there were more yoo yoo's, more dancing in the room but this time Jasmin sang: "AHHHHHH" along with the music! Miraculo, the kid does have a voice! My mispronouncing "an yousmi zarafa!" (My name is giraffe!) brought the house down. The nurses couldn't believe their eyes. There were three at the door now.

On a roll, we see Ophelia right after an invasive medical procedure and teach her three songs to help soothe the battle wounds. This lonely little soldier needs the distraction.

There are days when the "clown miracle" takes on a form that might seem "banal" in another context. They often happen when we are challenged by the nurses or doctors: "This child has not laughed or smiled in two months"; "He is in a coma, I don't think 'clowns' are appropriate"; "the mother is suicidal, I do not think she will tolerate a clown today" are just some of the things we have heard that can stimulate action on our part.

One of the nurses insists that we pay attention to a 5 year old named Elizabeth. She is just a glimmer of a child and has just come out of the Intensive Care Unit (I.C.U.). We have been told that her bone marrow transplant has failed and besides having a gloomy prognosis, she is in fragile condition and has not "smiled or laughed in 2 months." This information goes onto the clown hard disc and the old inner voices pipe up: "Jump off the clown cliff, girls. The parachute WILL open and you will land safely and not onto concrete." The moment we flash our red noses behind the window on her door we see Elizabeth who stares straight through us. Puffed up from her illness with a thread of blood at her nostril, she takes 60 seconds, then smiles and starts giggling. Unbelievable. Her mom darts out the door like a jack rabbit! Maybe her child's laughter was too much to handle or maybe she just needs to drink a cup of black coffee alone.

O.K. Rather than go into a poetic number that will probably do no harm, La Mouche, inspired, takes a risk. She lays a loud smack onto my Giraffe bum and then gives me a hard pinch. "OUCH"! A 3 Stooges-fever possesses us and we become a Broadway hit for our audience of one! We have a slam, slap, swat clown party for the next fifteen minutes! Elizabeth watches everything. She laughs, hoots, haws and almost pees in her bed. It is hard to believe this reaction after all we have been told. I confess to using some "popo" like techniques: BIG, STUPID, RAW gestures and actions, but this is an emergency! La Mouche is the incontestable counterpart as she hides in the closet, making "scary" noises to bully "la Giraffe" in the most sadistic ways. This is not tricky! Elizabeth desperately needs to see another "victim" besides herself and that is clear from the giddy-up. The harder the "auguste", Giraffe, suffers, fall and wails, the louder Lizzy laughs. The more confused and frightened the auguste is of her powerful, yet loving white clown, the more Elizabeth takes pleasure in our monkey business. As we sashay out the door to her applause, Miss Lizzy coughs up a Kleenex full of bright red blood and then looks at us as if to say..."maybe this is worth it..." Feeling like I have just killed a child, worried and guilty, I grab a nurse out of the hallway. She reassures me that the blood is normal, in Lizzy's present state. Nobody is mad at the clowns. I am still worried about the kid.

9.

"Balmy"

It is our second week here and Mimi claims the weather is balmy today. This morning in the day clinic, we invent a test called the "babe-o-gram" for a new 17 year old patient and according to the ancient osteo-humorology text book, it works! Actually, the girl is about to go for a scanner and is nervously getting ready by rummaging through her small suitcase to decide what she should wear. As if it really matters, but it does. Nightgown or sweat pants? Mini skirt or silk kimono? Lipstick? Blush? To ease her frenetic preparations, La Mouche and I simply "redecorate" her room with all the contents of the "babe's" bag, putting underwear on the television set as a hat, a bra over the lamp shade, like giant sun glasses. We love her orange lipstick and try it on. The place looks like a hurricane has hit. Hurricane GIRAMOUCHE! Girls, girls, girls! La Mouche claims that the room, too, is now dressed up, relaxed and ready for action! OOOPS!!! Here's the stretcher-bearer and ooolala, is he a hunk! See you later babe, try not to ruffle the young man on the road to the scanner.

Walter doesn't scream today but he looks at us like we are witches. I think we'll wait some more before we even blow a bubble.

The intern chases after us to say that Jasmin's face blossomed from a chalky white to a flushed pink after our session today. Wonderfool that even she notices. Better that she tells us! All we did was take goofy group Polaroids for Jasmin to send back to her brothers and sisters in Morocco. Then Mom invites us to Casablanca, for "when all this is over." Imagine La Zarafa (that's Giraffe in Arab) and La Moucha in veils, riding camels, eating fresh dates! Yooyooyooyooyooyooyooyooyoooooooo!

It's party time in Annie's room. Since she is in remission now, she and her mom offer us coconut cake and rum punch to celebrate their leaving for the tropics tomorrow. I hope they don't come back. Hic. Time for lunch. I better not do this too often.

Before eating, we are ambushed by a dozen nurses, interns and doctors. Have we done something wrong already? To our utter delight, they go down the list of patients, and want to know exactly how each one has reacted to the clowns. Even the Professor is impressed. This variety of gratitude is almost too much for us. We're not used to it. Maybe the clown transplant is beginning to take root.

Ophelia will be staying in the B.M.T.U. for the next 6 weeks, so she's going to need tons of attention. Her mom sent a supply of cassettes with ballads from the 60's and some opera: Maria Callas, Pavarotti. For a 9 year old? Ophelia talks to her on the phone at noon sharp each day. We're told that granny can't bear hospital life so we won't be seeing her for a while. The nurse on duty says that Ophelia watched a video of E.R.

six times in a row yesterday. (It's that soap opera about life in a Chicago emergency room.

In France: "URGENCES") I love E.R., all those sexy doctors (yum-yum). This shared passion gives us glorious food for gossip. So after a solemn discussion about "Carter", one of the T.V. interns, we get Missy to stand up on the bed to wiggle and twist! She already knows "Zizi pompom pompom" by heart, a L.R.M. standard from our "Haitian" repertoire.

Louie and his dad lie in bed together, looking like lazy sun bathers on an Italian beach watching girls in bikinis. As soon as we appear at the door, without missing a beat, Lou shoots smelly socks in our direction. This is a clear invitation for the cowgirls to dance to his pistols! After throwing most of his spare laundry around the room and 5 minutes of wild creative nonsense later we perform the world's first human body transplant: we take instructions from Mr. L. and transform him into his father and then the father into Louie. We might be grand magicians but Lou is Houdini reincarnated! Isn't this is a grand way to leave the hospital, in someone else's body? The kid is a genius and a great escape artist.

Her charismatic papa is "on the case" today patiently reading to Rosa, who has horrendous mouth sores and won't talk. This is one of the secondary side effects from chemo. We find out that she wants to keep her B.M.T. "bag" as a souvenir. Where does it go? In a scrapbook? On the dining room wall? We see dad later on in the hallways and take a picture of him with Giraffe ears. That'll be another "transplant" souvenir.

We initiate a new game based on our past success with Booboo, the monkey, where La Mouche tortures La Giraffe. It's clear that Rosa, like Louie, needs the violence in an innocent form. It's another 3 Stooges moment. Wham! La Mouche slaps me. Whonk! She rams my head into the wall. OY, YOI, YOI! This is the worst Popo-like clowning mixed with the overtones of a lamenting grandma. (moi) This style of clowning symbolises everything that is mediocre: no finesse, over-acted, too loud. But what do you want? It's helping an otherwise miserable kid have some fun. The big over-exaggerated vocal and physical "lazzi"2 work! So, these bits are working giggle miracles on Rosa. She is active and seems to be releasing a ton of anger and frustration in the play. Experience suggests the more a child suffers, the funnier he finds "clown-as-victim" games. Dad rolls his eyes and seems embarrassed. Later in the dressing room, Nadine makes loudmouthed fun of my new techniques and threatens to tell the other clowns. I'll get her back...

10.

3 Little Words

The weather lady says: "Storm warnings and high seas. Prepare a lifeboat." Ben's parents are on edge, especially the mom. The doctors told them yesterday that they cannot cure their 18 month old son. We haven't even met this family yet but it's all we need to hear. Even though we do our best to avoid running into her, mom "shushes" us three times. I wish I was invisible. Four times.

The reality of performing 50% of the day in surgical masks is beginning to weigh down on both Nadine and myself but we don't have a choice. Half of our comic expression is obscured, it's difficult to take a full breath and our smiles have been forced to migrate to our eyes. Some people only have their eyes to speak.

During the daily report, we are told that one of the pre-teen boys shaved his head over the weekend, to beat the fall-out. He looks terrific.

Before putting on our costumes, we make an inclownito visit to dear little Walter who finally releases a wee smile. This strategy helps small children to feel less threatened, and to make the transition from Nadine to La Mouche and from Caroline to La Giraffe. However, later, when we are "in clown" he cannot connect us to the 2 "ladies" he had seen in the morning and screams.

In costume and after the weather report our first stop of the day: the head nurse's office to sing her a few accordion classics from the 40's: "Three Little Words, Blue Moon"... This introduces more clamour into the hallways as well as ballroom dancing. Are they ready? After all, we are performing "authorised noise" for the queen bee and she loooooves the squeeze box.

At a distance we see Jasmin waiting at her door. Can't miss those eyes. "Aram Sam Sam, Aram Sam Sam, Goo li goo li goo li goo li - ram sam sam....." Her reedy voice weaves itself into ours but we feel that she is a thousand light years away. Our little Moroccan desert flower has entered a bleak medical tunnel and will go for a series of tests. The doctors think something cataclysmic has occurred in her lungs. We leave the room with a promise to take her on a promenade "around the block" on Monday. Mom wanders the hallways like a ghost skating silently past other parents, barely breathing.

Rosa is flat and depressed. The mouth sores persist. Dad cordially invites us in expecting more embarrassment. Not wanting to disappoint him or Rosa, La Mouche picks a fight with me as an alibi to rekindle the "abuse la Giraffe" game. Once again, Giraffe gets her head bashed and smashed into the closet door. Rosa thrives on these "live" power game shows: "Mighty Muscled Mouche vs. Giraffe the Fat Laugh". The wailing is louder than ever and the whole ward apparently hears us! At first this kind of clown-kid bedlam can be perceived as upsetting when heard from a distance. It can be interpreted as a violation of the sacred silence or possibly a real emergency. After a few months of the "marriage", the nurses say: "oh, it's just the clowns...." We still might get some looks. As we leave, Rosa sits up in bed and throws her arms around her papa's neck for a cuddle.

We discover Louie in a state of hysteria, harbouring humongous fear before getting a Lumbar Puncture. It consists of sticking a long needle into a child's lower back and is done with a type of anaesthesia that doesn't put the child to sleep but does help him not have pain. He has refused to get the test done (wouldn't I too?), so the doctor left an anaesthesia mask behind for him to "contemplate." One way or the other, screaming or calm, there was no avoiding the eventual medical procedure. In an attempt to soften the inevitable, we jump on the opportunity to invent 1001 incongruous uses for the mask: a hat for mom; a walkman for Martians; a toilet for miniature monkeys etc. Louie mellows, letting himself laugh and play. Are we compensating for the awkwardness of another "team member" or just doing our jobs?

Afterwards the doctors make a point of pulling us aside to tell us that "all had gone well". We double check back to find a nobler and calmer Louie. He tells us that this test (L.P.) does hurt and that it *is* scary. Mom watches passively. This is beyond anything that life has prepared her for. Lou then threatens to give us a special test, invented just for clowns: inject long sharp needles into our eyeballs. He adds that this procedure is not to be done to his Mom, who looks thankful. The knight always protects his queen. This boy does know how to use his jesters.

Maurice, 6 years old, is new. He looks like Mogli right out of "The Jungle Book." Long, silky black hair and burning coal-black eyes. Bedroom eyes. Quiet and gentle. He and his papa got off the plane early this morning from Polynesia, both wearing hot weather sandals and shorts. In Paris, we are already shivering with the first autumn frosts and are seeing the leaves turn colours. Dad is a cupboard full of worries. Before they haul Maurice away for "The Full Monty", he offers us a thin grin. No doubt, he will come back sore and disoriented from all the procedures they are going to perform. Dad goes to pace the hallways all afternoon.

We walk in to see Ophelia with the phone plastered to her ear. She has been chatting with her mom for an hour and her head stayed tilted for 10 minutes after they said toodaloo. A tidal wave of exhaustion has washed over her. So much medication, so many exams, procedures, too much fever. Before doing anything, we ask her to close her eyes. When you tell a sick child to close their eyes, it can be a big relief for she does not feel like she has to talk or partake in the clown play. This is especially important when a child is feverish, in pain or exhausted. Some kids are overly polite and will force themselves to participate. We tell Ophelia to "enjoy the radio" and sing Mozart's "Nocturnes" and then "Angels and Devils", a theme song from a 40's movie. She's an old fashioned girl. Tight harmonies, warm vibrations. We leave with our hearts bursting for this child who moves us with her finesse, her surprising ability to listen.

So what will be on our menu next time?

If you stop to watch children at play, whether they are playing a game (Tag, Hide and Go Seek) or are involved in more spontaneous dramatic play (cops and robbers, playing with dolls) often they are lost in the moment of their play: a liminal state in which they are oblivious to everything and everyone around them. Their game or play is all important.

Clown-doctors help children attain this state through play and shared laughter. When a child (or an adult) engages in playful creative activity with the clowns they can become lost in a creative moment: one that brings together physical, intellectual, emotional and spiritual aspects of their being in a way that offers unique opportunities for transformation and some self-healing to take place.

Although clown-doctors are not therapists in the current modern western sense of the word, when they engage a child or adult in shared laughter they are potential catalysts for healing. Like the Shaman before them, they do not consciously seek to heal, but rather act as a guide for a patient's journey towards their own healing. For in helping the child to laugh the clown-doctor enables him to lift the focus from their illness. While laughter itself does not cure any disease it may act as a catalyst for internal physiological changes to occur, creating the potential for healing to take place.

While the actual connection between laughter and healing is rather sketchy, there is now general agreement that humour and the resulting laughter do have predominantly positive physiological and psychological effects on body systems.

Many researchers suggest that laughter helps to: reduce muscular tension; stimulate secretions which encourage coughing and expulsion of 'toxins'; increase production of Immunoglobulins ("chemicals" which help to fight infection); stimulate increased oxygenation of the blood supply, giving more energy to 'cope' with illnesses and their medical treatments; release endorphins to help cope with pain etc.

Laughter may also interrupt a downward psychological spiral that leads to illness. Studies suggest that sustained emotional stress, can cause deterioration in body cells resulting in such conditions as flu, common cold, coronaries, cancer and strokes. Also laughter may help to fight the depression, anxiety, anger, fear, and insecurity that often accompanies illness. When we laugh, we don't think about what is wrong with us, we simply laugh. Laughter may not be the 'best'

*medicine but it certainly helps people stay well and feel better when they
are sick.*

11.

Still able to giggle

This morning there's a 5 year old boy, Martin, who everyone knows but the clowns. One of the nurses calls him a "regular customer". The kid looks like one of those roly-poly dolls that never quite falls but tips and rocks endlessly. He is waddling down the hallways right behind is his rather pregnant mama. These plump ducklings splashed instantly onto our puddle of frolic. Mother and child. No formalities, no knock, knock who's there, just pure trust in absurd fun! Play, play, play! They are diamonds in the rough.

His dad opens the door so we venture three baby steps forward into Walter's room as he is chuckling with an elderly volunteer. "Patty cake, patty cake." Walter puts his fears on hold, suspends his breath for 3 seconds and before he can remember that he is afraid of clowns and shed a tear, we rewind and exit out the red curtain!

Rosa is out of isolation (and aphasia) so the plastic flaps are wide open. I can feel that there will be monstrous torturing of Giraffe again. This is getting ridiculous. La Mouche is a hero and I am becoming a voodoo doll. Dad plays emotional repairman, winking at me and soothing me with his sympathetic words, the whole time taking photos of our brawl. Wonder what the album looks like out of context? Is he stealing memories for later? Parents do that.

Louie is out of control and demanding. He's begging for "limits" so we resist playing his favourite game where he throws stuff at us, books, toys or papers. It does crack him up. Reminds me of what mom said of my baby brother Josh when he was a 1 year old and hurling food onto the floor from his highchair. Some parents would just wipe up the mess or scold the child - my mother analysed everything, "Caroline, he is telling us where he wants to be...." Now here's the fool's analysis, Lou wants to get the hell out of that room. After all he is the great escape artist. I still get smacked in the head with a stuffed orangu-tang.

They are coming to take Jasmin to the I.C.U.. La Mouche and I stand at her porthole saying bye - bye butterfly with our peepers and blowing kisses to the wind. She opens a helpless eye and her kisses come floating back. Merde, merde, merde.

Ophelia lost all her hair yesterday and was not in the mood for song and dance today. All she wants is to show us her photo album of plump baby pictures, mama and poppa standing in a vegetable garden taken before her mom's accident. Then come some shots where the wheelchair appears and we see a blond woman with a 7 year old on her numb lap, Grandma sitting in the flower bed and more goofy family pictures. She needs to look and look and show and look some more. To remember the sensations of home: the smells, the colours, and the taste of her auntie's lasagne. A cloud of nostalgia perfumes the air. Ophelia, La Mouche, Giraffe are lost in remembering; dreamy girls. Intoxicated. Ophelia decides to play one of her mom's tapes. Barbara! We have to be patient and listen until the end. Then plan that next time we will make a tape of all "our" songs that we sing with Ophelia to send back to mom. Before drifting away, our little trio sings "Ira Congo, Ira congooooo, Ira congo bye-aye....".

One step into the hallway I suddenly remember my best friend from summer camp Becky, who played the oboe and who died of a brain tumour. We were just 13. I also remember that we had been birthday sisters. Until now I have buried this trauma and can't get myself to share it with Nadine.

Maurice, the new boy from Tahiti (who we also call Mogli) is blossoming like a rose, responding so quickly to our silliness that I thought he'd pee in his pants from all the laughter. Though he isn't primarily verbal, his eyes twinkle with 3 thousand thoughts and he is an exuberant tease. When I introduce myself as "Gi-raffe", he calls me: "LAAA- PIN"! (French for RAAA- BIT) I reply: "No, GIII-RAFFE!" He answers again: "LAAA-PI!" Me: "No, GIII-RAFFE!" Maurice: "Nooooo, LAAAAAAAA-PIN!" This cracks up Nadine who rats on me to the nurses.

It occurs to me that Maurice might have what many modern day psychiatrists call: "resilience." It describes that capacity to "bounce back" and to cope with trauma. Why some children can survive the worst situations (war, incest, hunger) without life long psychic damage, whereas others, even with a good prognosis and a good home, seem to shrivel up and let go of life?

On a quick break in the lounge to get our bearings, I share this with Nadine: Last night I stayed up watching one of those classic documentaries on survivors of the holocaust. This program was about the 1000 children who left Buchenwald alive thanks to the efforts of an anti-fascist German underground network. They all lived in BLOCK 8. The interviews were tedious and emotional. We have all seen this variation on a film a dozen times. I hate watching them; always cry, yet I can't help myself. They are addictive. One interview shone through all my tears like a diamond. A 57 year old man who had been only 4 or 5 years old at the time of his captivity, spoke of his happy memories at Buchenwald, something he felt difficult to admit. In his interview, he rendered homage to a young man, Valentine, who had been "in charge" of keeping the children out of sight and out of trouble each day. Valentine, had been a young clown with a Russian circus before the war. He joined the resistance, got caught and was sent to Buchenwald. In the concentration camp, all the children were slowly starving to death and meals were minimal, far spaced, but all the same, "an event", something to look forward to. Every day, to keep the kids from thinking too much about their next meal (everyone was so hungry), Valentine would juggle anything he could find: stones; rags; shoes. He'd make silly faces, create games and tell stories, to remind the children that they were still capable of laughter.

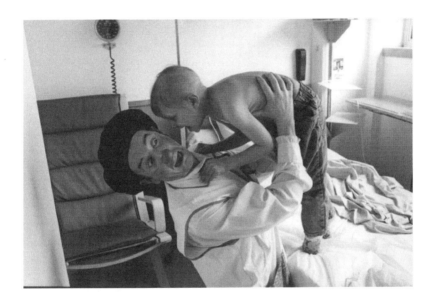

12.

Bobissimo

Nadine is on tour so it's time to weave a new colour into the cloth: Dr. Bob, Yann who has recently joined Le Rire Medecin. This is to be his first day of training. Such a pup, too.

Hospital life is mostly female; women outnumber men by the dozens. Moms predominate, so do Grandmothers and aunts, 90% of the nurses are female and so are about 50% of the paediatricians nowadays. I insist on hiring as many male clowns as female to keep a balance in the company as well as to offer the many advantages of male clowning to the hospital population. It's exhilarating to see the instant flirt effect on the nurses, mothers and even some kids. I recently heard a 6 year old girl wail as La Mouche and I entered her room: "I want a booooy clown, not a girrrl clown!"

There's fresh excitement in the air as we got the nurse's report. Even though many asked about La Mouche, you can tell that a male clown is just what everyone wanted. A sassy comment on Dr. Bob's hairy legs puts at least 4 nurses into a giggle fit.

Dr. Bob seems to have a civilising effect on Louie. He just needed a "boooooy" clown. This is the first time I see Lou stay focused on one thing. The guys race imaginary motorcycles all over the bed while I play super mechanic for the road accidents. Dr. Bob looks like he is having more fun than Lou. They make a real pair of ball scratching buddies. The grandparents sit like expressionless bookends, not helping, not hurting.

We can take our surgical masks off in Rosa's new room as she has been transferred out of the B.M.T.U. . To celebrate, I hope to introduce a new improvisation theme. Alas, violence is still on the top of her list. I take advantage of La Mouche's absence and slap Dr. Bob around. Rosa doesn't seem to mind this new role for me as long as someone gets victimised. She still needs the turbulence and Yann learns one of his first major lessons in clown-doctoring: a hospitalised kid uses "play violence" as a tool to channel pent-up fear, frustration, anger, boredom, even loss and sadness. What a sap, if he only knew of my "battered" past with la Mouche.

We hear a rumour that Elizabeth and Jasmin might be coming back from the I.C.U. . We miss our girls.

The curtain is open on little Ben's door. Before mom can say BOO, I play "Au Clair de la Lune" as Dr. Bob blows kisses with Lili, the mouse puppet. Surprise, surprise, Ben waves and mom relaxes letting herself feel proud of her son's bravery. Even a little wave can be a huge accomplishment for a weak kid.

Event of the day in the B.M.T.U.: "Justice of the peace" Ophelia, wearing a multicoloured crocheted hat (3 cheers for granny!), performs a marriage ceremony between la Giraffe and Dr. Bob! A nurse stands in as the bridesmaid and the stuffed Ladybug plays the best man. After walking down one meter of aisle, and almost knocking over the I.V. pole, with toilet paper for a veil, the bride glows with rapture whereas the groom is secretly arranging the divorce for next Monday's R.D.V. . Ophelia will play the lawyer. Marriage is a favourite improvisation theme that comes up periodically with seven to twelve year old hospitalised girls. Romance is splendid medicine for all ages.

Maurice calls Bob an "EL-E-PHANT" and continues to needle me with "LAAA-PIN"! When we ask him who Maurice is he replies: "I AM THE WIIIND!" This blows the air out of us and sends me home preoccupied with the meaning of life on earth, even a short one. How does a child cope with illness and when he cannot, how does he create a way to escape it. What is Maurice really saying? Does he mean to tell me that no one will ever catch the wind? That the wind has its own laws and that the wind can escape illness? It blows softly or it roars and howls, destroying the earth, disguised in a tornado or a hurricane costume. "The answer my friend is blowing in the wind. The answer is blowing in the..."

The wind can also empower. Last week an angry boy and his mother arrived on the ward. He was giving his mom a terrible time and looked so thorny that neither La Mouche nor I wanted to get anywhere near him. He had just found out about a relapse of his leukaemia and Mom wasn't in a tip-top mood either. At 20 feet down the hallway, I hollered to him: "Don't you come near me. Don't even BLOW on me and don't even think about blowing on my delicate clown partner!" An impish smile appeared as the boy puffed up and both of us went flying down the hallway to splatter onto the walls. He laughed. Mom cried. Once again, the power of a metaphor spoke volumes.

13.

Trust

This is Dr. Bob's second day and we fools are holding "court" in the reception area, using it as the village square for at least an hour. While Mimi answers the phone, everyone and anyone who crosses our path is cajoled into participating. A mom, who is usually laden with a backpack of sorrows, twirls in a waltz with the dashing Dr. Bob while her 13 year old daughter does a belly dance and I play the "Blue Danube" on the flute; Rosa's papa recites a Victor Hugo poem wearing my Giraffe ears; there is some zippy hide-and-go seek action with a new little boy; a lab technician does her own ballet version of "Swine Lake" as parents and children check in and check out, automatic doors open and close. We even see Elizabeth's mom watching from afar.

An hour later, at the request of a nurse, we play music attempting to help Rosa through a painful disinfecting scrub of her broviac, but we are superfluous. She is in a rage and the music probably feels like emotional blackmail. Only her papa succeeds in calming her, breathing tender words into her ears. Horse whispering. We leave with our tails down.

When a medical procedure is well done, it is the art of science. I watch the nurses in the day clinic perform a simple blood test and there is sheer magic contained in the concentration of the 2 healers; a relaxed confidence while the skin is pierced, just once, on the first try, with a minimum of pain, ruby blood rising into the syringe; the child looking at his vein. The precision of the gestures along with the flow of blood.

Unfortunately there is a certain violence to most of the "routine" medical tests that are inflicted upon children, an actual invasion of the body. These tests are indispensable for their treatment: the Lumbar Punctures, myelograms and blood tests. The nurses and doctors often have a cocktail of powerful feelings consisting of personal guilt and a noble sense of duty to help heal these little people. The kids are sensitive to the emotional state in which a nurse or doctor enters his room. Sometimes the patient will grin and bear the pain of a medical procedure just to protect his medical caretaker. Other times he will use fear and anger against the caretakers just to evacuate pent-up feelings. This can be misinterpreted by the caretakers if they take it too personally, then they enter cycles of unnecessary guilt.

I can recall one of the most extreme reactions I saw. A young doctor yelled sternly at a little elf who was weeping with fear before a L.P. She was being held by two nurses in a sitting position doubled over a pillow at her belly with an anaesthesia mask plastered to her face: "Shut up, so that you can relax!" This was almost as violent as other stock phrases we often overheard during a treatment: "This is for your own good. Don't you want to get better?" Luckily these incidents are rare nowadays. Nevertheless, it reminds me, even in these circumstances on how we need to reach medical caretakers in the most positive way possible. Clown-doctors cannot leave any room for misinterpretation or defensive reactions. Co-habitation requires that we avoid judging our medical colleagues, the invasive procedures and their occasional blunders. We make enough of our own. And a clown always says he's sorry.

The sun comes out in the afternoon when a "party" is spontaneously organised in Rosa's room. We manage to rope in at least 10 members of the medical team. All hell breaks loose at the expense of the white coats. Bob and I get them to squawk, flapping their arms like chicken wings, dancing like penguins while Rosa and her father glimmer in the limelight of our merriment.

While Grandma roosts quietly like a plump turkey, a game is invented especially for Louie where I show him how to "operate" Dr. Bob by using the T.V. remote control. Magique! It sends Bob smashing into walls, speaking in tongues, jumping like a frog and shooting imaginary outlaws. Lou adores the sense of power and choice this game gives him over our slapstick and how he can create his own comic accidents. This improvisation is a classic with boys ages 7-12 who have been caged too long. As we leave the room, Louie starts muttering like De Niro in "Raging Bull", "I'm the boss, I'm the boss, I'm the boss!"

All clown doctors in L.R.M. work extensively on switching roles as quickly as an aerial artist flies from one trapeze to the next. A great master (white clown) is the best slave when the tables must turn. A great slave (auguste) makes a superior master when the moment is appropriate. The clown-doctor must learn to skilfully "obey" or to "command" in order to serve the needs of each child and still keep control over the situation. Travelling from Rosa, to Louie to Ophelia certainly keeps us flexible.

Ophelia is now out of the B.M.T.U. She decides that Dr. Bob and I shouldn't get the "divorce" after all and that making a tape for her mom is far more important. Oh so casually, she mentions that her mom can't use her hands. So who turns on the tapes? Dad takes the opportunity to have a coffee down in the lobby. It also feels like he wants to leave so as to protect Ophelia's time with us. That it was something private, just between her and her clowns. What a prince.

Maurice continues to tease us. Mainly he insists that he is THE WIIIND and that I am still LAAAAAPIN! His trust in our clowning is growing. We play a jazzy pantomime game with him where each move becomes "contagious" and gets imitated or transformed by the next player who is touched. It is a fast ping-pong of rhythmed loony gestures. His dad won't participate but watches us from his armchair as if he were watching a football game on T.V.

Before writing up the day in our clown journal, we are invited by the Queen Bee to her office to drink champagne in honour of her birthday. I play her favourite tune on the accordion, "Three Little Words." She says she is going to print out the lyrics for the Christmas party. I guess that means I will have to bring the squeeze box and entertain the masses. Our Professor abhors the vile instrument and I loooove an all day party.

14.

Clouds

This week Nadine is back. I missed her. The unit is under a black cloud. "Don't know why there's no sun out in the sky...stormy weather." Everyone is worried about our darling Elizabeth and Jasmin fighting for their lives in the I.C.U.

The staff is becoming interested in the ways we can work together. We participate in two separate medical procedures with a nurse. Both experiences are challenging. In both cases, the kids are screaming bloody murder and the nurse seems uncomfortable and troubled by their fear. With Martin who five we are able to distract him quickly from the pain and the dread. Soft music. Just riding the wave with him. Not moving too much. Eyeball to eyeball. Afterwards he claims: "I want to thee (he has a lisp) the clowns everyday even when I'm fed up and it hurts."

For Rosa's blood test, we are helpless, just like the last time. We persist with gentle singing but decide to leave. There comes a moment when you must stop or you risk overburdening the situation with too much information for the nurse, the child and the parent. Rosa needs to scream. Even her dad is helpless today. She is fed up with all the medical procedures and since her relapse cannot tolerate even the smallest of pokes. Upon leaving, we can feel our relationship with this nurse grow and deepen despite our failure to help. Without speaking we have acknowledged her difficulty in being the one who gives injections, wipes tender spots and must do invasive procedures on children. It doesn't matter if we are efficient or not. The goal is not to make Rosa laugh, it is just to help her cope with the procedure. We show her that we accept her in any situation - screaming or laughing, tired and fed up, cute and playful. This is all part of what we can share with the medical teams. Acceptance and clarity are essential ingredients in the hospital marriage. When we all remain clear on who we are to the kids and accept what our respective limitations are, this reinforces the unity of the team without widening the gap between the "good" people who encourage laughter and the "bad" ones who hurt with needles.

Louie is making big time play progress with us! He invents a scene where he claims that we are dead! Using his new computer game, "Lara Croft", Lou tells us that Lara is "us" and then proceeds to make us watch him "kill" Lara in all sorts of ways with machine gun fire, hand grenades, sharp knives etc. When I say, "I don't want to die", he softly replies: "Watch how I can save all your lives." He is so sure of himself and completely immersed in the game, lost in the safe world of play. Like a noble fireman about to pull a screaming woman and her baby out of a burning house, he repeats the rescue scene at least 10 times while we peer over his shoulder oooing and ah-ing! I am fascinated, but I'm not sure La Mouche approves of getting killed so much.

Just as we are finally leaving the room, Lou cries out for us, appearing at the door with his mom and gives us a bag of candy for "all the other kids". What a surprise of generosity. It hits us hard how lonely he is, how much he needs to communicate with the other kids and wants to know who they are, to let them know that he exists, that he too is sick, that he too is "in prison" and that he loves to play and eat candy. He just wants to be normal again.

We check with the nurses to see who can and cannot eat sugar which is incompatible with cortisone treatments. 50% of the kids are on a sugarless diet. Then we proceed to distribute the bon-bons door to door, even to staff, along with a reminder to say, "thank you" to the big Louie.

We hear that Ophelia's mom made a visit over the weekend. She calls while we are in the room and thanks La Mouche for the tape, saying that she was "filled with happiness just hearing her daughter sing." We feel a strong connection to this mystery mom in a wheelchair. Will we ever meet her? This time poppa stays for the fun. He encourages Ophelia to send a thank you drawing back to Louie for the candy.

This is where our troubles begin...

Giraffe delivers the drawing to a Louie who is flushed with joy. He whips out stickers and crayons, creating an elaborate drawing saying "Thank you Ophelia for your drawing, I love it!" So, go fetch again clowns, go! "Woof, woof." We immediately trot down the hallway to carry the precious parcel!

It's getting contagious, another kid, Jeanne 12, has decided to write a letter to Ophelia. Bow wow! All this isolation. Windows are beginning to open up, or so it seems. Is the ice finally melting between the rooms? Maybe we are on to a new phase. Or is this just the tip of an iceberg? Despite the medical necessity for isolation, can't the children be allowed a minimum of "social life"? When they are out of the danger of infection, too often no one remembers to encourage them to meet others and to explore the ward.

We have opened Pandora's box by creating the clownette mail delivery service. After Jeanne wrote her letter to Ophelia, La Mouche decides that it is best to read the contents, just in case. It says, in a nut shell: "Dear Ophelia, I have leukaemia which is also cancer of the blood. I am getting a B.M.T. soon and I will fight for my life. What about you? Please write. Sincerely, Jeanne". No hearts, no flowers just the low down on her disease. Dilemma. We can not deliver the letter but we can not, not deliver the letter. Have our honourable intentions of de-compartementalizing space in the ward gone too far? What if Ophelia feels medically threatened by the information in the letter? Can that wicked virus also attack her? Could it kill her? What if her dad doesn't want her to know she has leukaemia? Believe it or not, some kids don't realise that leukaemia is cancer, or even a life-threatening disease and some parents hide medical facts from their children. Even teenagers. Worst of all, could this letter possibly cause Ophelia to lose hope for a cure? What if, what if, so many what ifs. Are we becoming too serious, like adults?

But we are adults and professionals, so we go seek advice. After a frustrating debate with the psychologist and an intern, who is at her wit's end and has never imagined handling such a situation. As I lurk in the hallway, La Mouche takes on the responsibility of asking Jeanne if she will modify the letter and omit the "medical" facts. Despite our apprehensions, the kid seems fine about it all and immediately takes out another piece of white paper and writes a whole new letter. But something is wrong. Nadine and I are unhappy and embarrassed about this. A powerful lump that tastes like betrayal is caught in our throats.

After five minutes of relentless teasing me with: "LAAAAPIN! LAAAAPIN", Maurice now baptises La Mouche, "MAD-AME" and a volunteer, "GRAND-MAAA." When we ask him who he is today, Maurice looks at us with one of his fierce dead pans and says: "I'M A ROC-KET." So not only does he want to blow away like the WIIIND, but he wants to launch out of this place like a space ship. He and Louie would be good co-pilots. I'm not sure what to think. I know, don't think, stay in the moment.

There is an inner tube of silence around Ben's room. The curtains are drawn again. To avoid causing trouble, we don't go anywhere near his door. That mom has enough to handle. Noisy clowns can stay away.

At the end of the day, Elizabeth arrives from the I.C.U. on a stretcher, worn down and shaken. One of the nurses tells us that she has requested "her" clowns. We sing delicately, in a whisper at her bedside and though she won't look at us, we know she is listening.

15.

Wings and Stars

Pessimism is brewing. According to the nurses, a few kids are sprouting wings. Death often loves a season. Nurses tell me that all the time. Outside on the hospital's grounds the autumn leaves are falling. Does pain hibernate in the winter and do tumours grow in the spring?

The nurses are requesting more classical music and say how wonderful it is now just to hear the flute or our singing duets while they prepare medications in the nurses' station. Sometimes I like to place myself, armed with a few Bach sonatas, at the end of a hallway and play for an hour. In the Bronx days, there was a young doctor who used to bring his flute every Thursday and we would set up in the hallways to play classical duets (Telemann, Mozart, Bach). That would make the kids howl with laughter to see a real doctor play real music with a clown. In this ward the staff is ready for us to augment the doses of serenading and interaction; they understand that they deserve moments of pleasure. It's time to go beyond stealing a moment for a cup of coffee or a cigarette in the courtyard. Why not sing with La Mouche or dance with the charming Dr. Bob?

Louie wants to show off his new behaviour. He is changed, displaying an amazing attention span now, an uncanny ability to focus on one thing at a time and has become highly skilled at the "Lara Croft" computer game. Grandma claims that it is designed for 12 year olds. In other words: see how my 7 year old grandson compensates for his illness by being a wunderkid! It's strange how some kids need to perform for us, wanting us to play the role of spectators. So, we take a balcony seat and watch how Lou manipulates all the weapons and kills 10 varieties of bad guys. Finally, he gets stuck trying to find the "dynamite that will blow up the cliff." So, we leave him to his merry frustrations.

It's lunchtime and Rosa won't take her medication before eating. Nad and I discover three desperate nurses, attempting 273 flavours of bribery to get Missy R. to swallow those two pills. Nothing is beneath us: La Mouche offers to buy Rosa off by threatening to lock La Giraffe in a dark closet if she, Rosa, ingests the first pill. I hate the dark, as an actress, a clown and as a person. With cheering from the nurses and protesting from la Giraffe, Rosa downs number one. So, into the dark closet I go. Bang, bang, bang! Then La Mouche generously volunteers to pour a quart of ice water over my head if Rosa agrees to take the 2nd pill. In the mean time, I'm yelling from my black cell: "DO NOT TAKE THE PILL, DO NOT TAKE THE PILL, Rosa!" To no avail. Number two goes down the hatch, La Mouche liberates me from the closet and it is "Niagara Falls"! I hate cold water and always scream when it gets poured over my warm body. So I wail, I scream and I shriek. Rosa is ecstatic to see someone else suffering "worse" than her! She loves all the collective theatrics and the mise-en-scène. The nurses are having a ball and I can tell we'll be pals soon. In the meantime I need a change of dry clothing.

The whole time I forget (we have been told this morning) that Rosa has a pernicious infection in her lungs. Do I really want to know that?

It is time to do my space cadet number for the new adolescent in room 202. Momo (Mohammed) has just been diagnosed with a "curable" form of leukaemia. He's an Arab kid from the hard suburbs, just turned 18 and has recently flunked out of high school. He comes from a huge family and has a chip on his shoulder. I make him my special project. I adore a new challenge. You must work quickly and precisely with teenagers and you have to sincerely love them. I've had one at home to study. From the looks of this Momo, there is no way I will last more than 10 seconds before he throws me out, unless I decide to go all out. I slink in like a Brigitte Bardot-Marilyn Monroe combo and say in my best Mae West voice: "Baby, baby, baby where have you been? Ooooooo, we were supposed to go to the movies last night and I waited alone at home by the phone for hours.... oh sugar, where were you and what *is* that foxy eau de cologne I smell?" I race out the door before he opens his mouth. This is terrorist clowning. Momo must feel like he has landed on Mars. La Mouche and a nurse are listening in, giggling out of sight.

Maurice's (Mogli) walls are bare and there are no playthings. All the other kids have an abundance of dolls, stuffed animals, drawings, letters and cards. This upsets Nadine so much that she stomps off to the head nurse's office to find a few donated toys for Maurice. The haematology and oncology units receive cartons of gifts for the "poor, sick" kids all year round, not just at Christmas. Why is it that people "favour" kids with cancer? The adolescent ward or the dialysis unit hardly ever get a thing.

Upon seeing the toy truck and teddy bear that La Mouche proudly presents to him, Maurice turns away and ignores her gesture. All he wants to do is tease me and play with his sheets. After all he comes from a modest fishing village and has probably always just played with what was around: sticks, piles of sand, shells. Maybe next time I'll tell a story with a special "La Mouche" pantomime, the one where she rearranges most of the room's furniture.

Ever since coming back from the I.C.U., Elizabeth hibernates all day long. We stick "surprise" iridescent stars onto her sheets for her awakening, a sign that we have visited. We hear from the nurses that the doctors have tried everything and now will stop "treatment." With this kid, there are invisible strings attached to each heart in the unit. It seems that when Elizabeth has a good day the nurses also feel good and joke around, but when she has a mediocre day they get depressed and schlump around.

Most of them have known her for three years, since she was a toddler; they changed her diapers and laughed at her first mispronunciations. We are all in an open state of denial about what is happening. Maybe it's the only way to cope.

Jasmin is also back from the I.C.U. with a 10% chance of survival. La Mouche holds her hand as only La Mouche can hold a hand while we sing in tight low harmonies. Five family members crowd around and Jazzy manages a real smile.

I wish we were allowed to visit "our" kids when they get sent to the I.C.U. . It would mean continuity for all sides. But the head doctor said "no." And then no again.

We are surprised to see 2 year old Ben who is hanging out at the end of a hallway with his mom. He must be is better shape to be out of his room. With one look from Nadine we know it is our chance to make contact. Speed can be a factor when a delicate task is to be tackled. This is the clown marriage at it's best. Without consulting each other, we keep distance on the fragile pair as La Mouche whips out the bubbles. Giraffe plays an innocent "Frère Jacques" on the flute and takes a 6 inch step towards them. I put the instrument aside to "eat" a bubble, burp a bubble, squeak a bubble, then 2 bubbles, 3 bubbles, catch one on my tongue and pretend to swallow it. Burp! Ben is mesmerised, then giggling and mom is melting like milk chocolate in our warm paws. As we leave, they clap and shout: "Bravoooooo!" Just the 4 of us, no witnesses, but it felt like a mountain had been climbed. Simple can be huge.

There are many reasons why it is better for clown-doctors to work in pairs, some relate to performance. A solo performer, no matter how skilled he may be, is limited. Without a proficient, professionally trained partner he must either put on a one-man show, or put pressure on the child to be part of "his act." There is no one to suggest other ideas; initiate a new piece of business, create improvisational conflict, help reset the volume if he is too "loud" or too "soft", or at the end of the day, to discuss the day's events.

Successful clown marriages are defined by the energies, sensibilities, and complementary skills and rhythms of the performers, irrespective of whether a partner is male or female. One partner usually has to play the white clown nominally in charge of their auguste. For someone must act as the "parent" to their partner's "child" making sure that things don't get out of hand. Almost all skilled clowns can play either role.

The specific dynamics of the relationship between an auguste and a white clown are the basis for the clown couple's "lazzi." This creates conflicts which are often resolved through the simple act of a child's laughter. A clown marriage allows a child to simply sit and watch or, moderate, enrich and develop the action. Of course if he chooses to participate, he can be part of a clown team, often becoming the true "boss" of the action.

16.

Countless Metaphors

We're still in "Lara Croft" mode with Louie. Giraffe finds it addictive but La Mouche is beginning to find the whole thing irritating. Lou appreciates my enthusiasm and our company. I find everything about the game captivating. Even failure is fun because the player gets to start all over again. Lou has such passion about the weapons, makes careful choices each time an enemy is to be tracked and killed. It's like watching a 3 star chef pick spices and blend textures. Nadine feels that he is getting stuck in a labyrinth with a dead end, that we should attempt to introduce a new game. When we do try, our boy becomes aggressive, throwing the usual array of stuff and spouting the usual: "Pee pee, ca ca, fart..."

Then it hits me, that these games of combat might be a tool to understanding his treatment and his illness. This is the coping mechanism of the century for Louie. I keep thinking of how each weapon might represent the chemo, the antibiotics, the L.P.'s; how all the tests and traps in the game represent the challenges he himself is going through: the fear of death, the nausea, the fatigue, the fevers, the sadness to see his worried parents and the courage to confront the pain of medical procedures over and over, preparing for the unknown. The game offers countless metaphors.

Before leaving La Mouche asks Louie to make a drawing for Maurice. Just to spice up the walls. He takes it to heart, meticulously designing a crimson and golden sun, setting on a turquoise ocean.

Maurice cannot be reached. Maybe he can only handle one event at a time. He is sitting with a volunteer, concentrating on making a paper Halloween pumpkin. Upon seeing the drawing from Louie, he silently puts it on the wall and sends back a cut out paper fish. Bow wow, off we go again! Fetching mail! Delivering hope?

While we are with Maurice, Louie starts shouting from behind his own door, "Hey clowns, hey Maurice! I WON! I WON!" You would have thought that he was celebrating victory at the end of a war! I was personally persuaded that he had just blasted the hell out of some enemy army on the computer game site. These small victories must not go unnoticed for a sick kid.

Pursuing my role as the great seductress, I write a mushy "love letter" from La Giraffe-Cleopatra to Momo. I beg him for a R.D.V. in his room in a few days. The missive is hand delivered by La Mouche who continues to have nothing flattering to say about her blundering clown partner. We often play "Good cop, Bad cop" and Momo is not "fooled", he wants to be left alone. "Clowns ain't my thing, I'm too old." He does read the letter and cracks up. (I was hiding around the corner, savouring the tiny "victory".) We repeat this type of prescription 3 times in the day, each time inventing a fresh alibi to get La Mouche into the room: "La Giraffe is so upset. She is waiting for an answer to her letter." or "I'm sorry, Gigi is such a tacky fashion victim, she wants to look foxy for you, any suggestions?" Momo grunts while I plan the next "medication" on his humour prescription. Only three more days and he's mine!

Brief halt in Elizabeth's room. Almost no light; all curtains are drawn. Through her high fevers, she looks at us from another world. Soulful eyes blinking a few times to let us know that she does see us, that we can sing and that "now it's time to go, clowns..." Mom paces electrically, around and around the hallways, driving the nurses up the wall.

Our desert beauty is in too much pain for clowns. Jasmin refuses to complain and won't use the auto-medication morphine pump. Anyway, she's barely conscious. Mom discreetly prays on a rug facing east.

To our surprise Diane (17) shows up, our super duper girlfriend of two years ago from the oncology unit. According to the nurses' report, she has developed a brand new cancer. A secondary cancer can sometimes develop as one of the rare after effects from large doses of chemotherapy and radiation. The Professor will call Diane and her parents into his office this afternoon to break the news. This is one time I hate knowing before the patient. I can remember telling Diane about a year ago, "Go home, and don't come back!" This is a clown's affectionate way of celebrating a cure. Now I just want to bite my tongue, swallow those old words.

In her room, Diane tells us that she is "bummed out" about stopping high school so early in the year, yet thrilled to see her old clownettes. She tells us about a new sweetheart, and we sing some tasteless old rock favourites: "Teen Angel" (totally tasteless), "Blue Moon, A Thousand Stars in the Sky....". She and Momo might get along. Mom sloshes in with a stock of fashion magazines and snacks to get her daughter through the week of tests and procedures. These two are professionals at hospitalisation.

What is one to think upon seeing three jars of lemon-yellow hair gel on a bald girl's bed table? Since Rosa still wants to skin the Giraffe's hide, La Mouche invents a new episode for our soap opera, "La Giraffe goes to the Beauty Salon". Guess who plays the hairdressers? Guess who provides the head of hair? Not Rosa. For the next 25 minutes, Madame Rosa and Madame La Mouche, famous hare-dressers (Laaaaapin!) goop the entire contents of a jar of slimy gel onto my head pretending to create a hairdo that will make all the men on earth fall in love with me. It's about time. Since they won't allow me to look in the mirror, I keep asking: "Am I beautiful yet? Do I look tantalising? Will the Professor think I'm gorgeous?" The two monsters bite their lips, swallowing fits of laughter and goop away. I resemble something from an underwater horror film: a concoction between a sea urchin and a porcupine (on drugs). Dad, toujours ze prince of polite, witnesses the scene without a comment. With my makeover, a "star is born" as I prance down the hospital hallways to show off. At least it gives the nurses and Nadine some fresh gossip for the lunchroom. I recommend to everyone crossing my path to "make a hair appointment with Madame Rosa." Nad and I cannot figure out why that hair gel showed up. Back in the locker room, it takes me 15 minutes to wash it out to the music of nurse laughter.

We see a pale Ben on a stretcher, going home. He is definitely, definitely showing feathers.

Surprise, surprise, little Walter is back in the hospital with high fever and has requested the clowns! We enter armed with Lili and Lola, our twin mice. He hates them so they get banished and hidden rapidly in our underwear and that gets the old boy laughing again. Clown knickers are a big deal in Le Rire Médecin. They must be colourful and personalised. Each female clown has her own style (ruffled, polka dotted) and they get shown often. Male clowns with over-sized baggy pants also wear zany boxer shorts for when the trousers drop. Dr. Zen has a dozen secret pockets to hide various and sundry props: rubber chickens, bouquets of flowers, squeakers, etc.

Walter is now ready to listen with both ears and watch with all eyes while we jazz up nursery rhymes and dance our clown minuet.

Ophelia is back for a week of chemo and we can't seem to get in the door. She has been submerged with volunteers and teachers. There is always someone keeping her busy. We finally get a ten minute clown moment with her. She seems subdued, deep inside herself, in her own faraway land. After trying a few simple riddles, she hands us a response to Jeanne's revised letter. Was it a surprise to read: "Dear Jeanne, Thank you for your letter. I have leukaemia, do you? I relapsed after five years of remission. My mom is in a wheelchair and she only came once to visit me. Please write again. Yours, Ophelia"

"Ahooooooooo!", the mail conundrum has resurfaced and as Nad and I still have not resolved the problem of what to do, we are crushed. This time we go to our noble leader, the Professor, for another jaw-boning session. He listens attentively to us and says that it would be best to also have Ophelia modify her letter, leaving out the medical details which might upset other patients. "Play it again Sam." We know he is right and though we do not want to not face it, Nad and I decide that it is curtains for the clownette mail delivery service. Even though it has revealed the children's' immense desire to say who they are to each other and their capacity to handle medical information, we realise that we, the adults cannot not cope. Teamwork is sometimes simply acknowledging and accepting limitations. We clowns cannot cope with the consequences alone. Opening up new means of intercommunication for the kids would imply a different kind of commitment and a more precise definition of each staff member's limits of territory. Most paediatric units are not ready for this kind of upheaval and redefinition of their medical and social identity.

In the meantime we ask Ophelia to rewrite her letter. As Jeanne, she will understand but will the other kids? How can we explain that our mailbag is now hanging in the closet? It is time for the dogs to bury the bone. Maybe we should change our job to curators and stick to encouraging artwork.

17.

"Hallo, Miffter Momo!"

Mimi says the weather is "unpredictable, the electricity is on the blink but the emergency generators are working so you must get dressed in the dark and the children's lunches won't be served until 1 P.M."

Have all the fuses blown? For the atmosphere is terse and tense this morning. One of the nurses is in tears so I imagine that someone has died. Wrong. It's just the global stress. We have coffee with a depressed lot who feel like they don't do anything right: "We don't seem to cure many kids here and can't keep the dust off the top of our lockers." They seem perfect from a clown's point of view, but terribly hard on themselves. It doesn't matter who has yelled at them or who is not getting better, they are "our" nurses now and they have pushed the "help" button. We are definitely in phase. It is beginning to dawn on me that I am now committed to the children and their staff here and that there is no turning back.

After the coffee break, La Mouche and I make a plan and spend the day reinforcing egos and singing: "YOU ARE ALL ZE BEST, ALL YOU NURSES HAVE ZEST!"; we award absurd prizes left and right: An Oscar for Miss Osteo-humorology and The Golden Funny Bone trophy. To do any good, we have to lay it on nice and juicy. Too much would be perceived as insincere and too little could be taken for indifference. Nurses and doctors are such perfectionists and fear failure like the plague. So who cares for the care givers?

It's a classical music day (Bach, Handel, Mozart etc.) so we set up a music stand in a central corner, spending hours just playing flute and kazoo duos, letting the melodies float into hospital rooms, drift into clinics and filter into lounges. La Mouche takes care to knock the music stand over as often as possible.

A new 6 year old, Stella is wandering the halls, clinging to her mom's side like a clam. We haven't really met, as she has just arrived, another Caribbean island fairy. According to the nurses she has not uttered a word yet.

Our first visit is for Rosa, who is going home soon. We spend the whole time cooking and steaming "bye-bye" kisses in a huge "see you soon big, baboon" pot. This choice of play was a surprisingly tender surprise but I miss being a scapegoat already.

We have two non-stop sleepers: Maurice, who has violent stomach pains and dozes all day. We had prepared to take Polaroids for him to send home but it won't be for today. Also, Elizabeth naps endlessly. We tell her mom to come get us if she wakes even for three minutes. Maybe we need clown beepers for emergencies.

We finally manage to include Louie's Granny in an improvisation, but he becomes distracted by the computer gods. We try our hardest to keep the game alive, but the more we try, the crankier he gets. La Mouche, with her unique deep-hued voice, decides to set a few "limits" when Louie digresses into a pee pee-ca ca tirade. Kids always listen to La Mouche when she gets serious. Pas moi. He can't wait to make "Lara Croft" die, expire and perish on gargantuan metallic spikes. It is a bloody mess but what a catharsis! La Mouche says she is fed up with the two of us. Grandma takes her side and I give Lou a fat wink and he sticks out his pasty tongue.

We have a poignant moment in Jasmin's room while a nurse injects medication into the I.V. bag for Jazzy's persistent pain. She barely opens her eyes as I flute an a Acapella Bach sonata. La Mouche sits quietly holding mom's hand. Mom weeps freely. Our sweet nurse stands breathlessly, holding a spare I.V. bag, incapable of going on to her next task. Five women "suspended" and encircled by a satin ribbon of emotion. It is a matter of time.

Diane is frazzled and K.O.'d with the renewal of medical rituals. After her R.D.V. with the professor when he announced the news about her new illness she apparently spent the whole next day in the dark. Now she is programmed to get what we call "The Full Monty" (a gazillion tests) this afternoon and will be getting a heavy dose of chemo next week. Nadine thinks she will be cooked in many a sauce before they get through with her.

When we came into Diane's room she was glued to the tube, watching a soap opera about an alcoholic adolescent that commits suicide. It makes her laugh when she describes the scenes. After we persuade her to shut the infernal machine off, Diane reminisces about her Irish Setter, her passion for horses, her boyfriend, and her adorable baby sister. Everyone loves comfort foods. I love soft-boiled eggs with toast and Nadine loves salted butter on dark bread. Like Ophelia, like many kids, Diane was sharing comfort thoughts.

It's a grand reunion with Martin, who is back in the hospital for a week of treatments. We take a break to play music while the doctor examines him as his Grandpa looks on tenderly. He has come from a mountain village and taken over hospital duty for Martin's mom who is about to give birth. Grandma is looking after the other children and dad eeeks out a living to support the whole tribe. Illness can seriously disrupt a family's structure. We see it when people stick together and we see it when things fall apart. It's like petals falling from a rose bush.

After the examination, we enlist Martin to play our ringmaster and chief triangle soloist. His lisp makes all of the announcements delicious and hilarious. Dragging his I.V. pole behind, he follows us into Ophelia's room. "Mith Ofelie, thep right up and enjoy the Thow!" Ophelia immediately pops up from under the covers. We help her sit up and enjoy a skit created with the 5 year old roly-poly, sending her into gales of giggles. For a few short minutes she seems to forget why she is in the hospital and as we leave her, those beautiful eyes are shining again.

We point our noses towards Momo the Magnifique's room. I am not alone for my R.D.V. d'humour, I've goit two chaperones: La Grande Mouche and the Petit Tin-tin. One of the all-time stupendous clown tricks for "depressed" teens is to get a cute little one to put on a "show" for them. We "pull the strings" in the wings. Martin's got his work cut out for him. Momo is stretched out on his bed, getting a red-coloured blend of chemo, which resembles Hawaiian Punch. Looking like the king of Saudi Arabia, he is impeccably groomed, smelling sweet, dressed in an egg yolk-coloured sweatshirt and matching loose pants. (After all he was waiting for me.) As we enter singing "You are my sunshine, my only...", and before Momo can reject us, our secret weapon, Martin, trails in close behind. He enters like the grandest of ringmasters proclaiming: "Laaadiths Tand mithter MOMO, Pleath enjoy our Thow!" Then he gives a "Ting, ting, ting" on the triangle. As we go into an elaborate flea circus number, with those six-foot critters performing high wire walking and some audacious fire breathing, I see tender looks washing over my ghetto prince's face. A gush of infinite sweetness bleeds into his hardened mask. My thug, this fallen hooligan. Now that cancer has dropped a bomb into his life, there will be no more stealing cars for a while. The only drugs he will have now are medical plus a long list of "hospital" punishments and solitary confinement in his....room. As we parade out to the next room my good egg says: "Hey, you bozettes, I still think what you do, is for little snot-nosed kids. So go get a make-over if you ever wanna come back." Ting!

With Tin-tin in tow, we repeat the performance for Walter who takes the bait and lets himself take pleasure in seeing another "patient" perform. When we exit, he starts to scowl, makes tight fists and glares at his feet. Did he get mad because we were leaving? The anger is a sign of progress! He's getting attached to us!

One of the greatest gifts we can receive is when a child or staff member "clowns" behind our backs. Long after we are gone, Martin will probably continue the act, entertaining other patients, the staff and his family. I can already hear the nurses recounting another "Tin-tin story" over coffee. Because his status has changed, going from patient to performer (fool), the medical staff can see him differently now. As the clown's "little assistant", he has something to offer them, he is no longer just "poor little Martin", who has cancer. These are some of the resources, the tools for resilience-bank, that we can leave behind with the child for the hospital voyage.

Fools are probably the historical ancestor of today's clown-doctor and were known by many names (Buffoon, Jester, Parasite, Clod,

64

Clown(e), etc.) They had many "skills" including acrobatics, clever dialogue, contortion, juggling, magic, puppetry, story telling, exhibiting trained animals and tightrope walking.

At one point in history fools were separated into two kinds: "Artificials" and "Naturals" who, because they were thought to be immune to the devil's influence, could wear anything they liked, do anything they wanted and speak their mind without fear of punishment.

Clown-doctors have found ways to resurrect the natural fool's protection. For once a bond of trust has been established, they can do and say things to patients, nurses and even doctors that everyone else in the hospital would deem unthinkable. They do this by taking risks. They push the limits. In so doing, they shake up its hierarchy and protocols and indirectly serve the healing process.

18.

The Giraffe and the Dragonfly

I abandon Nadine and take a short vacation to get some rest and distance. I need to see an open sky. There are plenty of clowns to take my place.

Far away in the south of France, while I am hiking, forgetting the battlefields of the cancer wards, a peculiar memory materialises. The nurses, the doctors, the teachers, the clowns and her family all know that Jasmin is on her way to the heavens. Yet last week in the middle of the afternoon, Jazzy's mother goes shopping for her daughter. As La Mouche and I came in to clown after lunch, we see her weighed down with large plastic bags and showing her purchases to Mimi: a fuschia snow suit; 3 boxes of chocolate chip cookies; stylish loafers; and, the latest "BABYSITTER" Barbie doll, complete with miniature twins. I am flabbergasted. Why would she buy all that useless stuff? A snow suit? It isn't that cold out and it certainly isn't snowing and besides Jasmin will never go outdoors alive again. And cookies? Jasmin can't possibly munch on cookies now. Leather shoes? Slipper socks would have been a better choice. And Barbie dolls? The kid was mostly in a coma, so how is she going to play with toys?

High up in the alps, I start to realise something I had never imagined and start to cry. Like the "Hand of Fatima", these gifts for her daughter might act as a charm to ward off the evil eye and ward off more harm. And don't all mothers believe in miracles? With the snow suit this "good" mother will keep her child as warm as possible as long as she can; for it is an animal's survival instinct. Warmth means life itself. Maybe the cookies are for offering to family and guests who will be saying goodbye soon. It was the least she could do to honour those guests and maybe the sweets are also just to give Jasmin the pleasure of smelling - something she could still do, even in an unconscious state. And for the dolls, they are one last indulgence for a little girl who would soon stop playing on our sweet earth again. Babysitter Barbie and the twins? Barbie as the caretaker of 2 little imps. A way of saying: "My dear, dearest daughter, I will not leave your side now, life will push on after you decide to surrender your last breath. So play as long as you can, even in your dreams and don't worry, I will continue to live."

The path until now has spiralled with adventure. Sometimes I get obsessed about how I became a clown. Why have I unconsciously chosen this journey to the red nose? I remember my childhood as a spicy sandwich composed of five layers: hilarity, guilt, boredom, terror and rebellion. I was a shy and dramatically clumsy Jewish child growing up in an Irish Catholic suburb of Washington D.C. . At school I spent 90% of my time day-dreaming, pretending I was someone else, looking out windows where the world might be free of rules, where I could fly. If I could only make it to adulthood.

After college, in 1971, at the age of 21, I moved to France to escape the fast food culture and thus pursue my childhood dreams of daily doses of goat cheese and Baudelaire. It wasn't long before I stepped into the skin of "Miss Lili Ratapuce", a contortionist fairy-clown and spent the next 17 years in the streets performing and travelling the world with two theatre companies: "Le Palais des Merveilles" and "Pandemonium and the Dragonfly". The dragonfly was always me and early on an obsession with wearing large iridescent wings was kindled. As soon as I had made them I created a number where, rigged to pulleys and ropes and in a secret harness, I would fly over the heads of my spectators. As I stole hats and replaced them on new heads, I wondered what reactions this produced. It seemed as if the audience received an intense emotion of flight yet I felt newly grounded. Little did I know how these wings and voyages of lightness provided me with a metaphor that helped later in life to brave the onslaught of tiny angels that I was to face in the paediatric wards.

19.

The show must go on

I am back "home" and am content to see La Mouche and the team again. In my absence, Dr. April, was a sincere hit with the nurses and several expressed their gratitude for the programming of another "male." As Dr. Roger Chips says, "Behind the red nose, there is a man. "It's never a good sign when the staff gets over attached to "their" clowns. Not fun for the "replacement." It's a sign of health in our liaison to them when another collaborator can be accepted and appreciated. The nurses tell us that they look forward to clown days and tell new children upon arrival all about us. This is a great sign of a successful clown-doctor to hospital transplant.

The news this morning is catastrophic. Jasmin died last night. It is our first loss here. It leaves us speechless and stunned. For if we talk now, we will break down and cry. And if we cry now, it will be impossible to clown all day for the others, who need us. Do the children know? I try to put this death into a secret place where I won't have to think about it. For now anyway, until I can be alone and meditate. I know Nadine is the same, so are the nurses. We have no choice, "the show must go on."

Circus clowns have always been given the mission to interrupt other acts and to parody them, to amuse the audience while there is a changing of equipment or to distract them in case of a technical error or serious accident. We are not far from our big top cousins today.

The report continues. Elizabeth has shut down all communication and another boy is in critical condition. In addition to the usual 20 odd patients, there are 3 totally new ones with recent diagnoses for leukaemia which means three more sets of anguished parents. One of them, a 2 year old boy is still screaming bloody murder at the sight of anyone that doesn't look like his mother. In addition, Karen lost all of her hair the day before her 18th birthday.

The good news: Doctors Dora and Sam, new interns, have arrived for a six month residency. Nadine and I know them from past years on other paediatric battlefields! This means that they are clown-friendly and we don't have to traumatise them at a tender age. It takes at least two months before an intern can adapt to a new medical unit as well as interact and work with the village jesters. At first they think they have to keep a serious, straight face in our presence, especially when a Professor is on the ward.

We see Elizabeth quickly in the morning and she sits up, managing a few smiles, plays a banana maracas, and rambles on about how the "pipi tubes" are bothering her. Five good minutes is all she can take, so we leave to tell the nurses how she did open up.

Maurice is not evolving well. He's withdrawn and limp as a result of unrelenting stomach pains and is becoming bloated from all the medication. His father watches over him like a hawk. They both look so completely lost, exhausted and distressed in our white world of medical miracles. We play lightly, dancing "around" his anguish just making an effort to bring serenity and some colour into the room. I remember that I have a camera with me today but since I don't have the heart to make Maurice pose, I take a few pictures of La Mouche with papa. Maybe the snapshots will reassure the folks back on the islands.

This time Momo doesn't resist us and lets me use my charm to engage him in a discussion. Naturally, for added effect, I exaggerated the lilt in my U.S. of A. accent. He told the clowns last week that he thought "la Giraffe" was pulling his leg with a fake American accent and was thrilled to find out that I really had lived in New York City! He even talks to us about: how he had loved Dr. April's magic tricks; his life in the projects; how his brother was in the slammer; admitted that he "borrowed" a Porsche but didn't have a drivers license; and, said his only goal in life was: "Leave the hospital. I'm just waiting for it to happen." Not even the T.V. is appealing. Since his main activity is ceiling watching, I paste a dozen star and moon stickers onto the plaster firmament. "You guys are hare brains."

The doctors are hospitalising Louie for an emergency. After returning home for a short stay, he's now got a mysterious high fever and is in a rage, pissed off to be here again. When I inquire about old "Laura C.", both he and mom let out a elongated sigh for their computer system has crashed. Then Lou starts shouting a rainbow of insults at us. "La Mouche has bad breath! Giraffe has a stinky tail! Go jump off a cliff! Get lost in traffic. You both have fleas!" That's our boy! Mom seems embarrassed but it does help Louie let off steam by playing the meanie again.

Sometimes in the most unexpected and simplest of ways a mother will let her child know about the possibility of death. Almost 2 years old, Ben is just a tender blonde. Today, he sits obediently on his plump momma's lap in a room in the day clinic waiting his turn for chemotherapy. Madonna and child are calm, at home, watching "Road Runner" on the T.V as I skitter up playing "The Codfish Ball" on the flute. It's a big deal. La Mouche and I have not forgotten the break through last time. So, mom whispers into her child's ear:" It's Madame Giraffe and we know her. Look, don't you see La Mouche playing in the hallway with Walter?" So the T.V. goes off and they sing along to the music. That's ritual number one. Three songs later, it's ritual number two: Time for all of us to "say goodbye" so La Giraffe can move on to another child. I pick a crimson goldfish sticker out of my secret collection to place on Ben's tiny paw as a souvenir. He even let's me touch him. The sticker will remind him of our times together later on when things might get "tougher." It may even inspire our little "fishy" songs at a needed moment. "Row row row your boat..." I notice that there are opalescent "bubble" stickers that can go along with the fishes and now that he likes bubbles I ask Ben if he wants one. I get a polite nod. Mom doesn't miss a beat and says "That way darling, the tiny fish will get air from the bubble, because without air, he might die." How loving of this mom to use the air bubble metaphor to help Ben realise that the chemo could "save his life", but that it might not. I take a deep breath and side stroke to the next patient's bed to join my clown partner.

20.

"Choose life!"

The phone rings at 9 P.M. It's Nadine, sobbing. I breathe in deeply. Since I was working in another ward today, she gives me the news, which is bad, really bad.

All I can do is listen quietly. "Elizabeth is barely alive. Diane is going to need a B.M.T. to save her life. They will start looking for a compatible donor. I brought her two horse posters. Louie is in pain and the doctors don't know the cause." To ease my apprehension, I tell myself that this is just Louie's style to give the good doctors a challenge with mysterious causes for his suffering. He is my most delightful pain in the arse!?!

She continues: "Last night at 8 P.M. Maurice, our Mogli, "LAAA-PIN", convulsed and his heart stopped at midnight. Gone with the wind. No one knows why and there were no goodbyes. Besides the night shift nurses, Dora was the only doctor around, and took it hard. His dad flew out of France on the first plane with the small body." Our brave rocket ship blasted off. Mogli has returned to his jungle.

It's so hard to hear or say the word "death", even silently. As I listen to Nadine, I long to get this haunting sensation out of my system. I feel inhabited by the upheaval that this news leaves me in. After Jasmin's flight, I wasn't sure I could face continuing in this ward. Now it's Mogli's turn to soar. When I hang up, to calm myself down, I get sidetracked. Experience has given me a few favourite therapies to soothe the wounded soul: the movies, reading trashy novels, cooking a gourmet meal and loosing myself in the dictionary. I look up "dead" in the "d" section and discover a whole page of morbid and sometimes hilarious synonyms and phrases. Some of my favourites: dead duck; dead head; dead meat, deadline; deadpan; dead wood; dead of the winter, etc.! Encyclopaedia reading as auto - therapy. My scholarly ghetto-bound ancestors would surely have approved. After all my mother gave me the Hebrew name, Chaya, meaning, life. She had her reasons. Like Jasmin's mother she needed to protect me. My American clown husband, Dr. Meatloaf (Stephen), reminds me at least 15 times a year of the old Talmudic saying: "Choose life!" So, I have, I will, I do. Maybe life and death just balance each other. Ying - yang. Hot - cold. Laugh - cry. Swim - FLY!

I fall asleep remembering all the parents I have known over the years who faced the loss of a child. I know one mother, an artist and a close friend, who continued to paint her daughter's portrait each year, letting her "grow up" on each new canvas. And there parents ones who looked death straight in the eyes; others hid and cried quietly in solitude; some broke down with loud wails right in public; others needed complete denial. They all touched me with their immense bravery for they suffered the worst, most unnatural thing that can happen to a mother, to a father.

21.

Our small tribe

It is a funny day in the haematology ward. After the three deaths last week, the staff is in a navy-blue funk and all too quiet. Betraying their detachment, we can sense their unresolved feelings and baffling guilt over Maurice's death. A few even complain that La Mouche and I have not been loud enough. A good sign? Can clamorous music heal grief? In the locker room, despite their remark, we decide to start off "low key", building our day's clowning voyage according to the palpable atmosphere. We promise ourselves, to sing beauteous songs and to shy away from anything overtly burlesque: No cops and robbers, no Three Stooges, no marching bands.

Elizabeth's taut little belly has tripled. She sounds like all the dishes have broken in her lungs. In her particular way, mom tenderly scolds Lizzy for everything and nothing. I find that reassuring for life goes on when a mom can still nag her kid. We sang over her routine chidings, not expecting Elizabeth to even listen to anyone. She's not with us anymore, but we must not let her feel abandoned by the clowns, no matter what her state of health. Mom stays at Elizabeth's side and keeps her own brand of distance from us.

Louie sleeps off his fevers like a baby cub surviving a harsh winter in a cave. Spring is only a few months away.

We have an illuminating moment in the B.M.T.U. with Karen and the nurse on duty who takes care of her. Our clown and nurse business goes from theatrical horoscope readings to quirky talk about mothers and daughters. Each of us offers a comic childhood memory concerning her respective female parent. I recount how I once delighted in frightening my mom by pouring ketchup (to imitate blood) over my naked body while in the bathtub. And the time I pretended to faint at the doctor's office before getting a shot. A big smile brightens on Karen's face when she says, "I haven't been simpatico with my poor mom. After all, I've put her through one bout of anorexia and two bouts of leukaemia!" As if naughty kids use illness to punish their good parents or as if evil parents did something bad and then are chastised with their blameless child's illness.

Diane is catching a few winks, except for a short visit from an old flame. In the hallways, just before going into her room, we tease him hoping that he'll be capable of warming her spirits up again. The guy looks so disoriented, so uncomfortable. How we forget the awkwardness of visiting a friend, a girlfriend, the one you first kissed, who is trapped in the hospital, whose life is in danger. One of a clown-doctor's goals is to melt the ice for visitors, give the hospital a welcoming atmosphere. Hospital-ity! The marriage of hospital and vitality.

I notice that the drawing Louie had made for Maurice (LAAA-PIN!) is pinned up in the nurse's station. Touching. Is it a rising or a setting sun? How many "insignificant" objects or drawings get left behind after a child dies here? They seem to hang in the air like lost grace notes in our hallways, small totems that remind us of the kind spirit that stayed behind to keep teaching us to smile. To put one hoof in front of another.

Over a leisurely lunch with three nurses, Nad and I end up having an intense discussion about children and death. Each of us share our most intimate stories, bonding to each other as women, as mothers, as caretakers. Unspoken feelings, long buried memories flow easily down a mountain stream. We are a little tribe, safe for a few precious moments. Where is the fireplace, the warm spiced wine?

22.

Professor Pewpew levitates

Nadine is on tour with a cabaret show so today I work with Philippe, a.k.a. the honourable Professor Pewpew.

Louie is feeling his oats again and has prepared a computer game surprise for the clowns! In a mock wrestling match he plays one clown against the other. "Killer Ken Giraffe vs. Savage Sam Pewpew"! To Lou's contentment, Pewpew goes on a winning streak. The old and faithful battle of the sexes, boys vs. girls which is another classic game with the kids.

Sweet Momo, puts up with "his" Giraffe singing a love song as well as being told a string of tacky jokes that Pewpew keeps in his repertoire for older adolescents. Small doses will get us far.

Stella, the new island-fairy still hasn't peeped, but she floats behind us amused with everything we do in the ward and with the other kids. This little chickadee has an "Alice in Wonderland" vibe, as she wanders enchanted with each clown-event that she discovers in the hallways or the rooms. It's as if it's always "the first time" with her. With her natural innocence she'll make a great clown partner. We get her to play a full-fledged game of "hide-and-go-seek" with Ophelia who is in for a week of treatments.

Diane has been transferred to the B.M.T.U. for heavy-duty chemo. We gang up on Pr. Pewpew, teasing him about his height (5 foot 2 inches). He is a master at playing the irascible white clown which makes him even more ludicrous next to my noodle-like 6 foot altitude. One of his comebacks sums up our relationship: "I am not your teddy bear." After we smooth out his ruffled feathers, Diane wants to talk about her current boyfriend and how intimidated he is when visiting her. How much she yearns for a real date, even here.

What a treat to see Martin tottering in our direction! He helps Pewpew and me to teach three medical students how to fly with latex gloves. They are timid at first and don't dare move, probably sensing a big wig somewhere near. With Martin's inspiring example, which no one can resist, we give each of them a pair of surgical gloves to use as "feathers", to be held on the ends of their fingertips. In my head the elfin words of Peter Pan resonate, guiding me: "Just think lovely thoughts, Giraffe and uuuuupppp you'll gooo." How we soar, how we flutter, glide and circumnavigate the unit in all directions. Dozens of eyes watch this strange parade consisting of three baby-doctors, one elated Tin-tin and two happy imbeciles with 12 pair of latex wings, running circles around the ward in a fight-flight for life!

After a month of voiceless silence, Elizabeth has hatched out of her eggshell. As she sees us peering through her window, she sits up in bed with excruciating determination. Oh, miraculo! We waste no time flying to her bedside. With enormous courage she says: "Ahhhhhh, it's so warm in this room. Clowns, I had a bad night. I wanted to pee and I hate all these tubes."

Imagine two dumbfounded clowns suspended on each and every of her 20 words. Now we were speechless. Noticing her stuffed teddy bear, wedged tenderly under an arm I say: "What is his name?"

> Elizabeth: "Mammy."
> Pewpew finally finds his voice: "How old is he?"
> Elizabeth: "5 years old, just like me....."
> Giraffe: "So, you like animals?"
> Elizabeth: "yes...."
> Pewpew: "Dogs?"
> Elizabeth: "Oh, yes." (this is not going at a fast pace.)
> Giraffe: "and cats?"
> Elizabeth: "The same..."
> Pewpew: "How about birds? Little pew pews? Like me, Pew

pew?"

> Elizabeth: "Nope..." She takes a long pause, gets a twinkle in her eye and answers: "They poo-poo everywhere...." Professor Pewpew almost levitated with wonder.

Had this conversation taken place with a healthy child it would have seemed banal and without interest, but with a little girl who hadn't spoken for so long and who struggled 24 hours a day to cope with her pain and her discomfort, in our book of clown doctor miracles it is a blessing.

Before moving on, we beckon a school teacher into the room who has been standing at the open door all this time, awe-struck at seeing and hearing the little one's desire to communicate. When Elizabeth sees her, she looks at us sternly and pronounces, "I would like to work now." The teacher rolls her eyes up, probably not knowing what to do herself. We tiptoe out, leaving Elizabeth with a wet-eyed school marm. Pewpew and I are touched to the rock bottom of our souls. Thankful for the gift but also thankful that we have always persisted in visiting Elizabeth even when she is under the covers.

As we are writing up our daily report at 6 P.M. tonight, a nurse listens in as we discuss today's oasis-moment with Elizabeth. The nurse says that until "experiencing it", she had never understood what our work was really about. Everyone in the staff had expected that we were going to be more "entertaining" as opposed to "useful." They had imagined that we would do innocent face painting, little group shows in the playroom and sweet balloon sculptures. She explains how intimidating and threatening clowns had felt to some of the staff at first and I am glad I wasn't too aware of that. Things are changing rapidly.

23.

Chic, another clown husband!

Dr. Chic, Dominique is my clown hubby today. He is a virtuoso on the slide whistle and carries around a pair of drumsticks to make percussion statements on everything from crib bars to bedpans. (Bed - pandemonium!) He moves like an eel and talks like a parrot! I have to balance that with the silence of a mermaid, the clumsiness of the goose.

Thanks to Mimi at the reception desk, getting the "weather report" each morning is an official part of our clown day. As if he has always done this, Chic asks: "Sunny?" and Mimi replies: "Yes, with a sprinkling of clouds, maybe some heavy winds blowing in from the hallways later this afternoon." Chic again: "Are we expecting rain?" Mimi: "Not today, you clowns can relax."

The nurse's reports are going smoothly. We still have three different people giving us "ze list", but we don't have to hang out and feel like famished alley cats pouncing on busy mice in order to get information on our current guests. There are some new kids on the ward and there's some noise about a possible national hospital strike.

Mid-morning while we are all saying good-bye to Ophelia, who was going home for just a week between treatments, she faints and has to be re-hospitalised. This is how she earned a prescription for 2 clown calls in one day! No appointments necessary.

Stella, our favourite caboose, is still smiling a ton of thoughts through her gorgeous silence. I brought in baby zebra ears for her to wear. Now we look more like family parading room to room.

Pow! Louie ambushes us in the hallways, using his breakfast banana as a submachine gun. Then he used an apple as a hand grenade. The housekeeper isn't keen on things getting too messy and let's us know with one dark look. Dr. Chic gets killed in 35 different ways so I get to play nurse and wrap 15 yards of toilet paper around his wounded red nose and various body parts. Then we all play Mummy and use up another two rolls of T.P.! Then we play Godzilla and top it off with a Superman extravaganza! Maybe we pushed it too far with the cleaning brigade. Toilet paper is one of the world's best props for a clown-doctor.

Suddenly I get a whiff of a lemon-lime cloud of perfume. I am convinced that Momo puts his after-shave on just for me, and O.K., a few cute nurses. Anyway, he really looks at me with pity in his eyes, but tolerates our good times together now. We now have a running gag: I berate his favourite nurse as much as possible and he protests as much as possible, defending the wench, fiercely. Since she really is such a beauty, I can come up with lines like: "Oh by the way, Delphine has grown a moustache overnight." or "Isn't it a pity that Delphine wears army boots and dyes her hair. She's not a real blond. Have you heard the latest "blond jokes?" Delphine accuses La Giraffe of having fleas, leaving hay in the toilets and stealing her boyfriends. (C'est la bonne guerre.) All is fair in love and in war.

Elizabeth's mom sees us coming and high-tails it out of the room. As we enter we slide quickly into a number invented on the spot just for Elizabeth. She watches attentively as Chic and Giraffe re-enact the "Nutcracker Sweet" on her bed using all 15 of her Barbie dolls and all her chocolates. Splits galore, pirouettes in mid-air and flying arabesques into candy boxes. Our cherished schoolteacher helps Elizabeth shake the pickle-maracas. For the grand finale we demonstrate for one and all how much Barbie's can do. For they make splendid mini feather dusters when turned upside down, can even fart, burp or have an "accident" on an unexpecting mother's head. Elizabeth laughs and applauds.

As I leave the room munching on a chocolate-covered cherry, I make a mental note to myself that there are three little words that still make Elizabeth laugh:" pee pee, poo poo and fart." Kids of all ages love these "naughty" words, but especially kids who are stuck with dysfunctional bodies. Wish she could meet Louie.

Lili, my mouse puppet, helps Martin through a long procedure, the cleaning of his broviac. Toujours the hospital "pro", he lays perfectly still, while his nurse takes care to wipe his sore skin softly. All the while our wild rodent "accidentally" knocks down everything in the room creating chaos and "peeing" on all the furniture. The focus is concentrated on the puppet so all we have to do is pull strings, making the mouse naughty. This way the nurse can "scold" us, taking on the role of the white clown, the one to re-establish order and "calm". Martin approves of her "authority" and laughs. After the medical ordeal, Tin-tin beams at both his nurse and his clowns: "Thee guys, I didn't even cry." That's when we all realised how much it really did hurt.

Diane is still blue: prussian, indigo, navy, cobalt and royal blue. An unexpected smile sets the room on fire when she speaks of her sweetheart. Since he doesn't have the courage to visit anymore and talking on the phone has its limitations, we encourage Diane join the 21st century and to hook her computer up for sending e-mail. Even Giraffe's return e-mail!

As one of the wisest doctors I know once said to me: "The day that you (clown-doctors) cease to disrupt us...is the day that you must leave the hospitals." This phrase has helps me feel bolder when provoking an "authority." One of our doctors (balding) turns 40 today and the whole team of nurses make a big fuss over him after lunch in front of Mimi's throne. Just by kissing him on the head, La Giraffe reaps a fine crop of blushes. Bald men redden splendidly, especially when 15 pretty nurses are watching. A few "hairless" kids peek out from their doors and giggle. They like to see us goof off and make jokes on the doctors. They need that. We know who the fools are, but who are the real kings in this joint? We were about to find out.

We proceed to visit almost everyone on the ward and reserve a half-hour to see the psychologist about Victor, to discuss his violent behaviour. According to the shrink, Victor is way beyond "playing" or using the clowns for catharsis. This 12 year old boy is in a dangerous rage. We have been ferociously ejected 3 times now and the psychologist doesn't want us to insist any further. We don't agree. Victor has been battling cancer for over three years. Now he is emotionally out of control, a veritable Scrooge, trying to terrorise everyone, wrapping his parents and staff around his little finger, demanding gifts from anyone who sets foot in the room. Most get booted out quickly. This kid must smell clowns because the moment we are anywhere near his room, I hear the lion roar. He receives a new toy daily from family members, but nothing pleases him. I can't help it, his persistent bad moods make me laugh. Reminds me of my father for some reason.

"If at first you don't succeed....". Risking a severe reprimand from the psychologist, with all odds against us, Chic and I somehow triumph in getting our "poor" selves into Victor's room. No dishes are thrown, and we do not give in to his whiny demands. We did not offer gifts. We just slip in quickly through the door and manage to stay for 5 long minutes. It seems like a stroke of luck.

At first we just stand up against the wall, not moving a muscle, not saying a word, blending with the scenery. Like garden gnomes in the bushes. Victor glares at us and he starts eating a yoghurt, real slow, taking time to suck each drop with an irritating noise. Despite the great physical effort he never lowers his stare. "Slurp, slurp." Stare. "Slurp." Suddenly a spoon drops and his eyes shoot daggers in our direction. Silence. This is our first cue to play the perfect "idiot-slaves." I rush over, bow to "His Majesty the King of Schlurp", dive under the bed, exposing my ruffled turquoise knickers and then silently, like Iras (Cleopatra's hand maiden), carefully cleaning it off, I hand the spoon to Victor. With perfect timing, my partner in crime, Chic murmurs: "Was that rapid enough for you, sire?" and believe it or not, Victor cracks up. I bite my lip, Chic stops all movement. Victor cracks up again. Then catching himself, he quickly regains a dead pan stare. We take a deep breath and leave before anyone thinks too hard, too long. We dart out the door and heard him chuckle again. This kid has a fabulous sense of humour, he was just holding out on us till we cracked the code. We just had a Victor - victory of sorts and couldn't wait to tell the staff.

This evening in the locker room, as I undress, I can feel the blood of the medieval fool rushing in our veins. We too, have allowed the kings to abuse and manipulate us for their own pleasure and needs. For our ancestors, kings and fools, knew all to well the thrilling role of wise and mirthful scapegoats.

Clown-doctors serve many purposes within a hospital. One of the most important is from time to time they act as scapegoats for the children, their families and even for the medical staff who work with them. Unfortunately this task, like making people laugh, has probably always been part of a clown's job description! As many a fool found out to his chagrin, it is a very small step from being the king's mascot to becoming his scapegoat.

In ancient times the scapegoat often was essential to the continued health and survival of certain communities and more importantly to their rulers. At distinct times of the year, people would feel that to appease the Gods or produce good crops, they needed to collect all their diseases, sins and misfortunes and bind them upon some hapless man or animal. Then they would kill the 'scapegoat' or drive him away from the community.

At one point a change occurred. The scapegoat was no longer a real sacrifice made to appease the gods. Rather the idea of killing the King became embodied in a ritualised performance, such as a Sword Dance or a Folk Play, in which an actor portraying a fool was killed and often later resurrected. At around the same time, the fool became institutionalised at court. His official duties included, "to jeer continually at his superiors in order to bear their ill-luck on his unimportant shoulders". As strange as this may seem, the fool was thought to be naturally lucky for it was believed, if you gave him your bad luck, he would give you his good luck.

To return to the hospital. At times anyone may feel the need to collect their "sins and misfortunes" and bind them upon some unfortunate; they don't have far to look, for at these times the clown-doctor is easy prey. They make too much noise. They are not always 100% sensitive to a nurse or doctor's mood (swing) and their irreverence can disrupt medical routines.

Like the fools who preceded them, clown-doctors seem to serve no useful purpose and are easily expendable. So why not project your fears, failings and general unhappiness on these "mirth makers. At those moments, the clown's value as a meaningful element in the continuing health of the community is forgotten. We are back in ancient times and the clown is not a human being but rather a "goat" to be sacrificed. However, unlike their ancient ancestors, the clown-doctor just like the Fool of the Sword Dance can be resurrected. For when they have served their purpose, their status within the hospital community is not only restored, but may be raised if the community or individual, like the wise king recognises his value.

24.

"In like"

It's still me and Dr. Chic.

The weather report from Mimi: "Calm with a few rays of sun shining through the grey clouds." Perfect day for doing "lots of nothing" or in clown code: a "C.R.M.". The term was inspired by a childhood memory.

In the saga of Winnie The Pooh, there is a moment where Pooh Bear (one of the greatest philosophers) thinks he has lost Christopher Robin, who Pooh calls his best friend. Tigger and Piglet try to console the discouraged bear by offering to be Pooh's "best friend, at least until Christopher Robin returns." Pooh thanks them by saying that they are already his best of best friends for with them he can do anything. It's just that with Christopher Robin he can do "nothing." And that is what may be described as a C.R.M.: the ability to be with someone and simply enjoy doing nothing and not mind. Unfortunately when encountering an ill child or their parents in a hospital, there is a tendency for professionals to need to do something with or for them, whereas, what may be most necessary is simply to be with them and do nothing.

In sharp contrast, there's lot's happening today! The hospital workers strike has hit full force: In the main lobby trumpets are blaring, whistles blowing, drums beating and angry speeches are being given over loudspeakers all morning. Hundreds of nurses and technicians will march down to the Ministry of Health in the afternoon. Our ward is a 'high priority care unit of children with acute illnesses" so the staff actually has to "work" even though theoretically they are on a boycott. They all have large pieces of tape on their backs saying: ON STRIKE....I write on my back: IN LIKE?...IN LOVE! and Dr. Chic: ON MY BIKE. Fools will be fools. With all due respect, nothing is sacred. We abuse everyone and everything equally.

Memories of being five years old come flooding into my brain as we waltz into Elizabeth's room. Three big pillows in home-made colours were under her back so that she is in a comfortable sitting position. For once, mom seems calm, sitting on a chair near the bed. Three I.V. poles are working overtime, dripping yellow, clear and murky liquids into our little princess's body. Mother and daughter listen with serenity while Chic and I invent a tale of two children who lose their way in a magical forest of birthday cakes.

One week in the hospital with persistent fevers is reducing our Louie to a subdued shadow. We find him relaxing with "Mammy-Fart" (his nickname for Grandma), just cutting out Christmas decorations. He cheers up when Dr. Chic starts shooting toys with a squirt gun. Chic and I get killed about four times each. On a better day we would have died a thousand deaths. It is gentle warfare and no one's stuffing is left strewn on the floor.

Victor's room is off limits today except for his mom and a chosen nurse. We don't even try to enter. We hear that he's been squirreling away extra food under the bed.

Momo is finally admitting to being depressed about ceiling watching and says he's out of steam. He wants to chat about his "tribe": How he and his brothers stick together protecting their sisters who must stay home and never flirt with the European boys; how non-Arab girls are just "candy" to him, to fool around with and how Muslim girls are for marriage and children, etc. Politically correct or not, we let him ramble. We're not here to judge.

We mosey down to the B.M.T.U. With her last drop of chemo for the week, Diane is in such a fine mood that she agrees to play Juliet in the "love at first bite" scene. I don my faithful Groucho glasses and moustache to read Romeo's role as Dr. Chic mimes all the other parts. He makes a splendid balcony.

Proud Martin announces that he has a new brother. A Polaroid picture is taped to the plastic curtain that surrounds the bed. Our Tin-tin is enraptured. We celebrate, joined by a nurse and a med student, with zany be-bop lullabies, loony tune dancing and getting the med student to treat La Giraffe for a chronic squeak in her heart. Tin-tin loves it when I play the sick one.

We run into a young chaplain sitting in an adolescent's room. I have never seen his fuzzy cheeks before. While he is doing his best to stay pious and unruffled it is clear that he is a green apple. Chic and I put every trick in the book to get a few stunning blushes out of him. Doesn't take much. We baptise him "Padre-Babyface." Luckily he loosens up and invents a clown gibberish prayer just for us. Religion, like illness is too important to be taken seriously.

Upon leaving, I bump into Diane's mom. She says that no one ever comes into the room to just speak about nothing. So many lonesome parents here and not enough "Christopher Robins" to go around.

25.

Cumulus

At last Nadine is back and our first act of the day is to get the weather report from Mimi: "No storms but a mixed sky, the strike is still on and I assume positions are hardening. Prepare your umbrellas just in case."

The day starts off with an intense discussion with Emma, who is responsible for the volunteer teachers that navigate the hallways, all with identical blue book bags laden with math, history and French. They are a small army going from room to room to entice the kids out of chemo fogs, fatigue and fever. Read, draw and write, it's all in the good school of "life goes on" in the hospital. There is sometimes an unfortunate conflict of interest when few kids are either available to be "clowned" or taught. We have the sensation that the new clown invasion hasn't been digested by the academics yet. It's a question of time.

The "dyspepsia" was confirmed last week, when Dr. Chic and I accidentally walked up to a kid's door and were yelled at by an old school marm swearing that "reading, writing and arithmetic would always be a priority over silly clowns!" This little "accident" happened in front of a 9 year old girl who was so embarrassed for us she didn't know what to do, or say. We did our best to save face and skate quickly in another direction. Normally, a rapid "noses-down" chat in a back room with the teacher would have solved the problem. But this public reprimand, in front of a child, had crossed lines that were not professional or polite. This granny was not going to budge or discuss anything. Hence the dialogue with Emma to work out the kinks. We try to get her to see, that as the new immigrants in the ward, there has to be more tolerance, integration and flexibility. If we are willing to respect and understand the academic space, are they ready to acknowledge ours? It's not a contest. We must fight fire with water, although I'm tempted to use ice cubes once in a while.

Emma listens and comes up with a logical solution that resolves the problem: "Since there is no use putting a cat in a bird cage, I will simply program Miss Cranky to teach on another day. Everyone can handle that, right?" This is how the gentle teacher earned her nickname; "St. Emma des Clowns."

We get involved in another conversation with the psychologist, who is new in the ward. We exchange more impressions about Victor and he admits to not having had much experience with children at the end of their lives. Since he is genuinely interested to hear of our own history with life and death, we suggest a few books to read such as the Kubler-Ross "encyclopaedia", Stephen Levine's meditations. Just another day in the life of "Dr. Fraud, the clown."

Collaborative work, with the physiotherapist in Elizabeth's room, pays off when she agrees to do one or two gentle exercises to our music. Everyone signs up to contend in our "make a stupid face" competition. Mom sticks out a long pink tongue and Elizabeth has a giggle fit! There is a 3 star clown recipe for making kids laugh: get a parent to do something wacky, like imitate a chicken dancing or scratch fleas like a gorilla. It never misses, especially with teens. Once a teenager said to me, "You are such a nincompoop, Giraffe, that you even make my mom laugh." That went right into my secret collection of thank you notes.

Slowly but surely Louie is pedalling his mood up hill. Jump starting him with a promise to give La Mouche a "shower" puts the twinkle right back into his eyes. After a few motorcycle races over the pillows and through the sheets, it is time to carry out my promise. La Mouche gets an unexpected glass of water poured over her head. She threatens to never set foot in Louie's room again without wearing a raincoat and bringing an umbrella. She should have listened to Mimi's warning.

There are mega-computer problems in Diane's room. Her mom can't get them connected to the Internet and everyone's snarling, feeling really disconnected. We can feel a balloon about to burst and we don't want to be there when it does. Zen, minimal clowns here. "Ommmmmmhhhh."

A fresh bag of bone marrow has arrived in Martin's room for his transplant. A brother is the donor. Now his picture is up next to the baby's on the plastic curtain. Dr. Dora, our intern admits with emotion, that this is the first time she has ever seen a B.M.T. . I've seen hundreds by now and they still smell like boiling artichokes. Grandpa is in a solemn mood during the drip. These B.M.T. days are always taken seriously by the families. It's understandable, when you know that it is a last ditch treatment to save a life. For Tin-tin, it's just another bag of gooey stuff, part of his routine for the last year. So we surf Martin's sweetness and play one of his favourite ritual games that involve producing squeaks from our various body parts. Grandpa does the crossword puzzles.

Inspiration hits as we meet Stella in the hallway. If she won't speak, then maybe I'll try whispering. For it might be a step in the right direction. We'll see. I have a plan. After I speak a few feathered words into her ears, she nods and starts running back to her room. Nadine and I follow and find her in the bathroom. She immediately hands us her mom's nail polish and her favourite baby doll. There always seems to be a few colours of polish around when we visit her room. Next comes my plea that La Mouche and I are so troubled by her silence that we are going to bite our nails to the bone; so to keep us from doing that we would both appreciate an emergency manicure and that it wouldn't hurt to prescribe the same treatment for the doll. Dolls get worried too. During the 15 minutes it takes to get the triple manicure done, we begin conversing in balmy murmurs, fragile beginnings of vocal communication. We heard her voice at last. Stella the star is talking!

Then, La Mouche gets a brilliant idea. She thinks, and Stella agrees, that the doll baby must go for tests. Stealing an empty crib on wheels, the 3 of us proudly parade around the village square 60 million times, making sure everybody sees us with poor miss baby doll. Mimi picks up the phone and "schedules" her for a cat scan with Doctor Felix M. (F.M.), the radio-therapist. Everyone on staff plays along. We collect fake blood samples to "take to the lab", a phony case history folder, and the capper: Dora, the best intern in the world, gives the doll a complete physical exam. Heart, ears and tummy. Stella watches her "child" like a mother hawk while I daydream that I'd like Stella or Dora for a mom in my next life.

26.

On the high wire

All the serious big wigs are in Montreal attending a conference this week. So the atmosphere is sunny and the village seems open to even more clown festivities. It will be a golden day with Yann, Dr. Bob. He is making impressive progress as a clown doc, fine tuning his energy to each child and situation. Plus it's nice having a young clown spouse.

Mayhem is created this morning as we are chased and pursued by Rosa who comes back to show off her newly grown hairdo (2 inches already!) It is so good to see her in decent shape. "I am the boss" (sounds familiar), she keeps shouting our way in front of nurses, housekeepers, parents, other kids, our young interns and residents (the future heads of paediatrics). She locks us into the doctor's conference room and decides that Bob has to pinch one of the female doctor's bottoms before being allowed to leave. Things get fairly rowdy for the unit and we even get a few more kids out of their cages and into the hallways. Louie flops to his belly, G.I. style to "machine gun" both Bob and La Giraffe each time we come spinning around the corners. During the mayhem, history repeats itself. Another one of the blackboard matrons yells, "it is impossible to work in such a circus-like atmosphere." Bob ignores her and does 100 "punishment" push-ups for Lou as she spits this out. Joy can be a violent feeling for the chronically serious. Some days I feel like what we do is on a social tightrope. We must gracefully cross to the other side without losing balance or falling on anyone's head.

Business as usual, I pursue my futile romance with Momo and naturally Bob takes the male-bonding route. Mo has the delicacy to wait until I am in the room, then asks me to look into his eyes, while he tears my latest love letter into shreds and throws the cloud of paper into the air. The Giraffe won't give up, even in a storm of confetti. Men!

Dr. Bob, the human juke box, gives Diane the show of shows in the B.M.T.U. She reveals that hip-hop dancing is her third passion in life, after horses and romance. It's great having a young performer. I swear that man knows every rap song on the planet by heart. I just keep putting coins in the slot (a pocket in his white coat) and a new tune blares out. Diane is in stitches as a crowd of two nurses gather.

What's the sound of 3 dogs barking? Bow wow wow! All Martin wants to do is play "puppy." One of our specialities. Not a human word is uttered during 10 solid minutes of solid woof-woof. Grandpa reads the sports section. The nurses think we're cracked.

It all starts when Elizabeth's mom starts to take a shower as we are entering the room. Things have been going so well with this mom, that we need to find a way to keep her involved with us. We are not going to let her escape to take a shower or have a coffee. So, gently pushing her aside, I rush into the bathroom to take "my" shower first. As I peel costume parts off one at a time, tossing them into the room from the bathroom, Dr. Bob starts dressing mom up as "La Giraffe". Somehow, in the next 10 minutes, we manage to disguise Elizabeth's momma as me, and Bob improvises a romantic scene proposing marriage. I have to stay in hiding in the bathroom as I am now "naked." (Not really) Bob varies his methods: standing on a chair; on all four's; under the table; rap style; ad infinitum; and with each refusal Elizabeth has gentle fits of laughter. It is good to see this momma engaged in play, her daughter enjoying every second. After this, Dr. Bob retrieves my stuff then joins me in the bathroom where we proceed to switch our costumes for the rest of the day. That really throws everyone. I take a Polaroid to leave with Elizabeth.

At lunch we have yet another long, involved talk with 2 of the nurses. They want us to tell them if we are performing in the real world and when, to bring fliers, put up posters and give them free tickets! As one of our 11 year old patients said today: "When I hear clown noise in the hallways, I try to imagine what naughty things you are doing and I'd like to know what you do when you're not here with us." After Yann and I finish writing in our clown journal, and he has left, I stay late just chatting with Mimi, Dora, Dr. P and the head nurse. It feels lovely to finally be part of the family. After such rich days it takes me hours to digest and calm down.

27

I'm dreaming of a white Christmas

The Christmas season is descending upon the ward with a flurry of paper holiday trees painstakingly decorated and autographed by each child. They float from the ceiling at one end of a hallway. The art teachers have been working overtime. Two, four-foot artificial pines with synthetic snow, stand as solitary witnesses in each corner of the ward. Nadine is back in the saddle. As a response to all the holiday embellishments we devise a plan to create wacky costumes to jazz up our routine. I make a list of stuff to buy: tinsel, metallic bulbs, some sleigh bells, etc.

During the nurse's report, I learn a new word: "idiopathic." It means a disease or condition that arises spontaneously, or for which the cause is unknown. I love it. I love it. I feel idiot-pathetic often; quite often.

The two of us walk 20 kilometres of hallway searching for clown victims. For some reason, the place has never felt so empty. Between the 5 teachers and the 3 volunteers, we have to go "kid fishing" and take some hostages along the way. Seeing less kids means that we can spend extra time with staff.

After a lazy morning, we have a raucous lunch with the usual suspects. The back room humour goes from chats about holiday recipes to even sex. A classic. I share a story with the troops about how I'd once smuggled a giant sausage into the U.S.A. This is followed by a lewd remark from a nurse at which point Nadine gets an uncontrollable case of the giggles and starts producing sounds like a seal in heat. When she gets that way, there's no stopping her and she has to leave the room. It's highly contagious stuff. No one can stop laughing for a long time. It hurts. We are exhausted. When a group can laugh together, they can cry together. Are we building credit?

As we open the door, La Mouche snaps: "Keep your trap shut Gigi and bottle up!" Elizabeth is wide-awake and can still giggle at our mock fights, despite new medical complications. She keeps busy making Christmas cut-outs with the volunteers avoiding all eye contact but still follows every move that La Mouche makes to trick La Giraffe. Sometimes sick kids have an incredible ability to compartmentalise activities so they can take in two or more things at once. I can't help but thinking that she is preparing to leave a few traces behind so we don't forget her.

Martin doesn't look great, his body is transformed by the after-effects of the B.M.T. His catheter is infected which means that any tests involving an injection must been performed directly into his arm. On top of it all, his veins are fragile and it takes the nurses a long time to find a "good" one for any shot. We arrive just after a interminable series of blood tests and as his nurse leaves the room Martin lovingly says to her: "I fink I wore YOU out today." Hearing this noble phrase, she looks at us like she might cry. Kids get skilled at protecting their nurses. So Tin-tin is tired and only wants to play from a lying position. This is the first time that he takes on an aggressive role, playing a growling tiger and clawing us from afar. It gives him some authority and seems to be just what he needs.

We spend at least half an hour with Diane, in the B.M.T.U. . Her clock is ticking loudly. She has that androgynous "Joan of Arc" look; a gorgeous kid with sapphire eyes and heart-shaped lips. The nurse on duty joins us for a long spiral of serious clownesque debates about life, death, love and hip-hop. Diane claims that her closest friends at high school have all been through arduous life experiences and that has helped them stick together. Two have fathers that died from brain tumours, one lost a sister to suicide, another was raped and as Diane put it: "we're not into the latest nail polish colours..."

We learn that Victor has gone home for hospice care. So we don't even get to say ciao or get kicked out of his room one last time. He began to like that ritual. Sometimes there is no closure.

28.

Clippity-Clop

Just as we are expecting a day of calm waters, Mimi warns us that: "the weather is going to be agitated." Nad and I put on our holiday duds: La Mouche in a white diaphanous ball gown as the Mistletoe Fairy and la Giraffe is decked out as a Christmas Tree, decorated with tinsel and 5 dozen multicoloured bulbs all a bobbling. Actually, I am a hobbling specimen of a sapling, having broken my baby toe the night before on an innocent chair leg. It's a tender moment when a clown-doctor gets either sick or injured. My foot is examined by our dear intern Dora, a cancer specialist. She un-peels my striped sock and declares the toe officially broken for it is a puffy violet-indigo. (Goes with my costume.) The compassion and attention I get from all the nurses and kids looking on, is a treat. Everyone has advice, even the children. It hurts like hell.

The place is jammed and despite my infirmity, we create hallway bedlam. What a thrill after Monday's gloom and stillness. Two gleeful little ones chase each other in and out of the day clinic before getting their Lumbar Punctures and chemotherapy. A 10 year old girl with Down's Syndrome races into the walls with a tricycle, while Louie is out to the end of his leash (I.V. pole), machine gunning everyone in sight. He even lends us a few toy guns to shoot at each other and at the nurse's behinds.

Elizabeth is making progress with her pile of Christmas decorations and asks us to take Polaroid photos of her favourite nurses, "to keep forever."

Stella, who has been mute for the last month, emerges from her silence and becomes our personal elf, following us everywhere and insisting on painting my nails a bright gooey red to match my nose. My cup runneth over. The kid is gabbing non-stop. In the space of a week, she has gone from silence to whispering to running off at the mouth. No one can believe their ears. Let's hope it continues. She demands that we stay in her room while the nurses take 15 minutes of blood samples. Then, she stops talking and does not make a peep.

In the B.M.T.U., Martin informs us: "Today, I am thick", his tummy hurts. Everything is relative. Actually the doctors are worried about his liver. To help him swallow three big pills we sing Christmas carols with him. When the phone rings, he asks us to sing: "Jingle Bells (Petit Papa Nooo- eeel...)" for his mama and the new baby. We often do phone-clowning when asked; it helps the child share us with their families.

By the end of the day, we have pinned a few dozen Xmas bulbs on white coat lapels, pink uniforms and I.V. poles. My dress is almost empty. By then, Louie has calmed down and is playing chess with his dad. He tells me, with a straight face: "By the way, Giraffe, before you leave for home, why don't you go rip all of La Mouche's hair out." He should talk, the bald rascal. Once again Lou is using aggressive tactics to cope with his loneliness, the limitations of his freedom, the bleak periods of isolation and the loss of hair.

There's a computer nerd in the B.M.T.U. setting up Diane's Internet connection. That's a priority so we promise her a double dose of clowning for next time, besides, the guy is not bad looking.

Like a petite queen in a wheelchair-throne, Stella goes chatting off with the attendant, to get full body radiation, I sit down at the front desk with Mimi to gab and get back into the mood to face life as an undercover clown. Nadine rushes off to pick her daughter up from school and I hobble home with my toe is throbbing.

29

April Showers for Winter flowers

Alexis, Dr. April, is back in the village of blue skies after a month's absence. With the Xmas trees now ready and decorated, the children are excited about the annual party coming up in a few days. For the umpteenth year in a row the same ventriloquist and magician will make an appearance before Santa gives out presents. A million and one wrapped gifts, all donations, are piling up in the head nurses office. Now who will dress up as Santa? Sam? The computer nerd? Not the Professor!

Ben is here again, still alive and he sleeps all the time. His mom agrees to wear a bright red Christmas ornament on her sweater. (I've got a few dozen bulbs in my bag.) At least she is walking around in the open, not sitting in his darkened room.

With a high fever, Tin-tin is not up for much except a little game of touching, dancing and tickling hands through the plastic curtain around his bed. Hands are the clown-doctor's best marionettes. They can go into any room, you can't lose them and they can be kept perfectly clean. They can squawk like parrots or belch like sailors. Plus they can blow kisses and get into fights. April is told not to move while I quickly check on Diane in the next room. Tin-tin likes the responsibility and the idea of playing prison guard. I can hear him say every few seconds: " No, Dr. Aphril, no, no, no, do not moofe!"

April and I don't want to get caught in another chit-chat trap now that Diane is feeling better. There's a time to talk and a time to play. Every one loves a victim, so we girls team up against my clown husband in an exuberant master/slave game. We get a frantic Dr. April to interpret a galloping horse, a drooling St. Bernard, Pinocchio spouting a Victor Hugo poem and a belly-dancing penguin. We run him ragged and are having a decent laugh until an x-ray machine, followed by two alien technicians, bull-doze their way into the room barking: "X-ray, clowns...out!" How delicate.

Stella, the mad-moiselle, now out of her enchanted closet of silence is becoming a real boss. She has decided that we are her clowns, her fools, her jesters. Leading a red-nosed parade, she feels free to indiscriminately pinch bottoms, get under skirts, sing and dance like a carefree, "normal" child! She hikes up her own dress at one point and shows us her massacred belly and chest where the broviac is implanted. The blue markings for full body radiation are drawn here and there and many scars criss-cross the surface of her skin. She will go for a B.M.T. soon. But the way she giggles and lifts her skirts we feel like it is "recess" in the school courtyard and the girls are teasing the boys by showing off their undies. The kid has such grace, such spontaneity.

For the record I count and record several major breakthroughs with staff today:

* In our morning parade, Dr. April and I were joined by a young intern playing the kazoo, a nurse shaking the maracas and a housekeeper blowing bubbles.

* A nurse asked Dr. Dora if a 3 year old, who has been in her room for forty days non-stop, could come into the hallway wearing a mask so she could enjoy the clowns. The nurse not only saw the benefit of the child playing normally, but Dora also made it possible.

* The staff is actively and regularly asking for feedback about certain kids. So we are beginning to give it to them more naturally and more automatically. They continue to be stunned by Stella's social progress and have many questions for us about her surprising personality turnabout. We are all grateful that she has broken her long rule of silence and is now playing interactively. I encouraged them to join in more so as to show Stella the playful aspect of their own personalities."

There are three inter linked areas of skill that are paramount in a clown-doctor's work: performance skills (clown-character, improvisation, music etc.); interpersonal skills (listening, reading the scenes, relating to medical staff, understanding family dynamics and children's developmental needs); and healthcare team skills (understanding their role, working knowledge of disease aetiology/ medications and their side effects).

In practice, for the clown-doctor to be successful, there needs to be a seamless flowing between these areas of skill, for none of these 3 exist in isolation. To be strong in one, or even all areas separately, is not sufficient. Just like the Master Chef, this requires an understanding not only of the individual ingredients at their disposal, but also how the ingredients may be combined, the taste preferences of the guests for whom they are cooking and perhaps most importantly, the limitations of the kitchen in which the meal is being prepared.

No two patients, no two hospitals, no two families are the same. This is where the true skills of a professional come in. He must listen totally, with all antennas up, read the situation, then choose an appropriate mix of business (situational improvisation, music, song, etc.) to meet the needs of the scene in a particular hospital room, with a specific patient and their family, and within the context of the regime of a hospital.

30.

Where's the Sanity Claus?

Alexis rings and wakes me at 7 A.M. saying that he has a high fever and cannot find another clown to replace him. It's the Christmas party today. On one hand, I have a strict company policy about never performing alone. It is a straight road to "burn-out." On the other hand, I have promised to visit all the kids who are not allowed to leave their beds to attend the holiday celebration.

I cancel the morning, but a solo Giraffe makes a showing around 2 P.M. Before getting into ears, nose and tail, I bump into Dr. Y., who looks like death warmed over. Expecting a calamity, but hoping otherwise, I imagine that a dose of Bugs Bunny will not make things worse: "What's up, Doc?" He is so pale and his breathing is so shallow that I start to get worried and embarrassed about my little joke. Then he mutters: "This is the saddest day of the year. Everyone is happy, the kids are getting loads of gifts and the parents are eating cake, drinking champagne. All I can see is the prognosis of each child staring me in the face and what the treatments are doing to them." He turns his back on me and trails off to an empty office to shuffle papers and to avoid the festivities. I wish I had been in Giraffe.

On that note, I get into costume and head over to the B.M.T.U. so as to avoid filling in for late ventriloquists or disorganised magicians. I doll myself up in a polka-dotted B.M.T.U. outfit and I have just finished the 5 minute hand scrub when the head nurse rushes in to root me out. I am just about to enter Diane's room when the head nurse requests my presence "on stage" and insists that I come play the accordion. I pray that the Professor isn't around. Naturally, by the time I get out of my costume and arrive on the scene, it's too late and the magic show has just started. I see half a dozen polite kids in masks, sitting in a row, looking like angels and 30 adults shuffling about impatiently while the Christmas fanfare commences. Discreetly I about-face and high-tail it back to the B.M.T.U. . I hate being alone.

I dress and scrub for the second time. Despite my efforts, Diane stays depressed and won't even talk. Martin feels left out and won't look at me. All he wants the magician to come to his room. Feeling lame and slightly useless, I keep it simple and stupid and then skeedaddle. Still glad I have come today.

I go to Elizabeth's darkened room and see that she is back under the covers. We don't even exchange a word, I just sing a few soft carols. Despite her sadness, it is heart-warming to see mom mingling in the hallways with the others, eating cake and even smiling. Sometimes people can be judgmental when a parent takes any kind of time for herself before returning to her vigil.

A few kids later, as I gallop down the halls towards the holiday snacks, I run into a pair of catatonic parents, staring out a window at the far end of the ward. This is a world of contrasts. Jingle Bells is playing hard and fast on a distant boom box. Kids, families, nurses and doctors are having fun and eating candy. Santa is about to make his appearance and these two souls are lost on a new planet. My three second diagnosis, seeing the stream of tears running down their cheeks, is that their son or daughter has just been diagnosed with something devastating. And here is a 6 foot fool in Giraffe ears, accordion hanging from her neck, flabbergasted with her mouth open. My heart takes a flying leap. In an awkward, spontaneous gesture to hug the mom, one of my squeakers goes off, the mouse puppet drops out of my knickers to the floor and my heavy instrument whacks into the dad. I cannot have planned a stupider moment, bittersweet, to say the least. We are three rainy-eyed fools who cannot help themselves from laughing. Thank god for these accidents. If only time could stand still some days.

31.

A Leek in the Oncology Ward

I spend the day in the oncology pavilion and realise how much this break is welcome, freeing me of the responsibilities that go with my own territory. Today, I can let my partner, Jean Louis, Dr. Loulou the Leek, do the driving. The spaces are open here, the children have more freedom to wander and I have years of history with the staff and some of the patients. This place was my "first love" when I came to France to start Le Rire Medecin. So much had to do with a certain Professor Jean Lemerle, the head of paediatric oncology at the time, who was the first doctor in France to open his doors to clowns and thus risk his "serious" reputation.

It is a glorious day of roaming around with Dr. Loulou the Leek. The amazing part of having a perfect clown mate is that all your performance skills get better. With an attuned partner, it's like holding hands and running at top speed in the dark, with confidence that nothing is going to hurt you. Sometimes our breathing patterns are perfectly in synch, our hearts in tune. Like lovers. From tender to exuberant, from romantic to pugilistic. One steps to the left as the other trips him and then catches him before he falls. At all moments your vision must be 360 degrees; you need 10 sets of ears. You must never lose your partner, even when you have locked him in a dark closet, slammed a door in his face or are pouring a quart of cold water over his head.

We have a tight power play between our characters that works efficiently. I can increase my level of innocence, so that Jean Louis can augment his salty side comments and grotesque mockery behind my back. The more La Giraffe swoons and knocks into objects, the more Loulou can complain, become exasperated or ironic, and then re- establish "order." We share many rituals and lazzi. Loulou will often threaten to put La Giraffe "in her cage", or to send her back to the Bronx Zoo. The "dunce" always gets a maximum of compassion from the kids. Most audiences adore frailty. We play loving, good cop, bad cop.

Kenny, a 4 year old cherub that we have all known for 2 years is showing most of his feathers. It breaks my heart when my nose is down. This kid is such a champ, boxer with his illness. We have had such raucous times. He knew just how to reject us. I can still remember him chasing us all over the ward, pulling Giraffe tails and teasing Loulou. Now he's sitting in a wheel chair, bloated from the last stages of his illness, bearing the side effects of medication and he's wearing dark glasses to keep the lights from hurting his eyes. I cannot help giggling thinking hoe he reminds me of a mini-white Ray Charles.

Loulou and I waltz into the playroom where 7 or 8 kids, including Kenny, are making Christmas decorations with the art teacher. A few parents, Kenny's mom, his two grand moms, and an older cousin are also hanging out. There is a sweet, industrious atmosphere. Here comes trouble.

As we parade in, I conveniently drop my pickle maracas, then bend over to pick it up displaying as usual, turquoise ruffled holiday knickers to one and all. Loulou reprimands me. Everyone giggles but Kenny, who yells: "I AM NOT AFRAID OF YOU MADAME GIRAFFE." Everything is silent. No one is sure what he means. We segue to a new tactic:

Giraffe: "Hey, you rascals all have moms here, I want a mamma too.....Will you be my momma? How about you? Will you be my momma...?"

Loulou: "Cork it you big noodle and go stand in the corner." Everyone is giggling.

Giraffe: " Pulllllleeeeeze, won't somebody adopt an animal? You can even take me home. I don't eat much. Just chocolate ice cream. And, I'm tall, I can paint the ceilings."

Loulou: "She's mental. I'll pay any one of you to take her off my hands...I'm fed up Miss Giraffe, go to your cage!" more giggles from the peanut gallery. Just as Loulou and I get into second gear, Kenny interrupts again.

Kenny: "YOUR PARENTS ARE DEAD MADAME GIRAFFE, BECAUSE YOU ARE A GROWN PERSON NOW." There is a long silence. Think quick Gigi, time for a reality check, Kenny is telling us something. Take a deep breath, stay in the moment, don't drop nose, answer directly.

Giraffe: "Listen Kenny, my real parents are thousands of miles away in America, they are old, and they are alive. The Giraffe just wants a momma here and now in France." All eyes are wide open on Kenny, what will he say now? Without missing a beat he yells at me.

Kenny: "YOUR MOM AND YOUR DAD ARE LYING IN A BIG BED NOW BUT THEY WILL GO UP TO HEAVEN VERY SOON." He resumes his artwork, the grannies freeze and his mom (in tears?) darts out of the room. Loulou and I take a low bow followed by a deep breath and parade into the hallways. There is no applause and no laughter. It's not easy to continue our clowning so we retreat to the nurse's lounge for a break. This is how Kenny carefully prepared all of us for the imminent separation.

When I go home I make a huge pot of chicken soup, call my parents, just to check and come down with a cold.

32.

Let them tears flow

A few days later I go to the Rire Medecin office and first thing as I arrive, my secretary says that Jean Louis has called twice already. When I get back to him, he says that Kenny spread his wings the day after we last saw him. This news does not surprise me after what we all knew was a matter of days or hours, but somehow it unhinges me. I fall to pieces and dissolve. Sometimes the departure of one kid symbolises the death of dozens of other treasured children and takes on volcanic proportions. You just cannot sweep the emotional shock of losing a Matthew, an Anthony or an Emily under the subconscious carpet and expect a holding pattern. On a cold winter day our Kenny has died. A whole dust-pile of mourning has blown up in my face, tears start to flow and I am drained again.

Since Jean Louis doesn't have the strength to call too many clowns, we share the delicate task; I first call Nadine because she needs to know, she was so close to Kenny last year. The news activates our company's phone tree. We never leave "messages" about a child's death on an answering machine. Only the human voice of a sister or brother clown will do. Sometimes a letter or sometimes a note in the clown journal can soften the news.

After one of my birds has left the branch, I will write to his family. But not always. Sometimes it's really too painful. When I do write, it's my last shot at closure. It means I haven't really said "goodbye." I never call. But today, I call Kenny's mom. Writing won't do it for me. I have to start the dialling three times. My fingers get stuck, I make mistakes. A feeling of panic starts to overwhelm me. She picks up. Words come slowly and tenderly. Our silences are stretched, yet not unbearable. We simply need to be connected for a few minutes. Two voices merely touching. There is no confusion about each other's pain: Kenny's mother's unbearable agony, a clown's heartache. She tells me about the church service for 2:30 this afternoon, over 400 kilometres away from Paris. It will be impossible to make it. Looks like I will have to lament in Paris and I do not want to be alone.

I have the intolerable sensation of being an emotional bowl of Jell-O. Plus I feel the urgency to sit peacefully and honour Kenny's short life, his family's struggle to endure the unacceptable and his passage from the earth to the heavens. Up to the end, his family believed that a miracle would keep Kenny alive. He died in the discreet space of 15 minutes when his parents left his bedside to make a call. This is nothing new. Kids look out for their parents and sometimes choose a moment to die so as to spare them the heartbreak of seeing them go. I've seen it many times.

I call Jean Louis and ask him to meet me at 2:30 P.M. sharp at the cathedral near my office, so that we could light a candle for Kenny. We need the ritual and we need to be side by side. Nadine says she will do the same in the town where she's on tour; we'll all be together somehow.

Over lunch with possible donors for The Rire Medecin, I get a secret pre-church urge; an impulse that only a Jewish kid from the Maryland suburbs gets while downing a hot sausage pizza: the necessity to recite the Kaddish later on in church. It's the Hebrew prayer for the dead: "Yisgadal, veyiskadach chemé rabo..." The beautiful ancient phrases sing and repeat themselves in my memory like a mantra, but will I remember all the words for later? It's a good thing my lunch guest can't read thoughts.

Mission accomplished, Jean Louis and I meet and sit for 30 minutes, lost in our individual murmuring, "Hail Mary's" mingled with the "baruch-atah's." It's all so simple and so unbearably sad. In these moments clowns get close to each other. When I get home, I light a 24 hour yartzheit candle. My family knows better than to ask why. As a child, we always lit one on the anniversary of my grandfather's death. The flame helps you to remember.

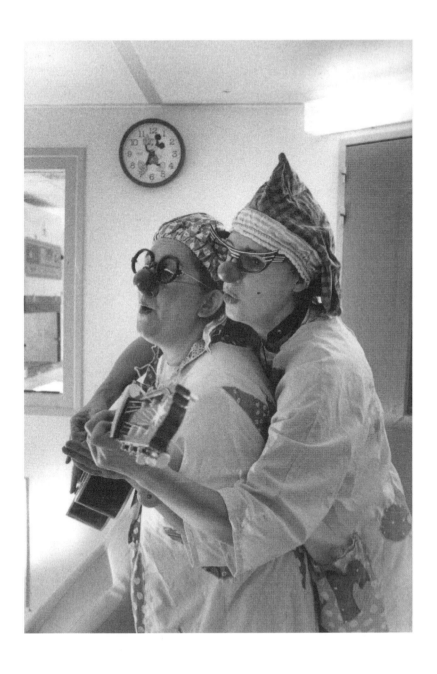

33.

Silent Night, Holy Night

Christmas week, a few years ago, in the oncology unit, Dr. Babycakes (Bernie C.) and I used to visit a 12 year old girl who was in a semi-coma. Her own mom had died of cancer the year before and her dad and aunts were always close by, supportive and attentive to all her needs. They did not lack in the humour department either. Clowns or no clowns, that family knew how to laugh. We called dad "Super Babycakes" because once he had swapped "costumes" with "our" Babycakes and also because of his Michelin-man corpulence.

Now that the kid was half moon-eyed, all we could really do is stand around her bed, singing her favourite songs and keeping some of our best running gags alive with her brood. I noticed a picture on the wall of a calico-kitten, sitting in the girl's lap. When I asked, "Oh, so you love cats too?" Unexpectedly two starlit eyes opened. Babycakes piped up: "Oh, so you ADORE cats!" Her round face started to glow slightly and she nodded. The family was stupefied. Me: "Listen, Super-Duper Babycakes, why don't you wrap that kitten up like a holiday gift and sneak her into the ward tonight?" Dad replied: "It would mean the world to my daughter to snuggle one more time with 'Twiggy', but isn't it forbidden to have cats here?" We left the room with a calypso bye-bye and a "we'll look into the kitten matter with the staff right away."

In the nurse's station, we were told: "Under no uncertain conditions can an 'animal' be brought into an oncology ward. It is strictly against hospital rules (of hygiene). But after all, this conversation has not taken place." This was followed by a glorious wink and a sigh. We went running back to Super Babycakes and whispered to him that operation "kitty cat" had been successful, BUT he must be completely discreet about the "Christmas gift."

Two days later, while getting the nurses report, one of them looked at Dr. Babycakes and me and just said: "meow", followed by an exaggerated wink and the whole flock of nurses giggling. Needless to say, a proud Super Babycakes met us in the hallway to recount how his daughter had "awakened" just enough time to enjoy Twiggy-the-cat's secret venture. He said he would never forget that moment, no matter what happened.

The holiday tidal wave is hitting hard. There are too many volunteers, too many parties and much too much candy. And the gifts. So many gifts. The head nurse is about to drown in piles of donations in her office: hand knit sweaters, Barbies, C.D.'s, wigs, stuffed animals, books and mechanical monsters. Louie will like that. There's not much for teens or parents. The staff performs the usual medical mambo and takes time out to fill up on fancy patés, chocolates and smoked salmon from thankful parents. We're all going to get a "crise de foie." (That's what the French call indigestion.)

I thank the laughing gods that most of the kids have been loaded up with a cocktail of miracle drugs that put them in a holding pattern. That should prevent a crisis. Now they can be sent home for a few days of grace and family festivities.

There are two new "diagnostics", with more parents in shock, trying to cope with the immediate blow and orienting themselves to hospital life at holiday time. There is no "how to" book for these situations.

Elizabeth is back in the I.C.U., we have no news about Ben (we might never get any more either) and a 16 year old boy (not yet a man) is being hauled off to the sperm bank; just in case the chemo and radiation treatments render him sterile. There's a good chance. For if he survives the illness, he might want to have kids. Has he even made love yet?

Momo is burning daylight watching Godzilla movies. We share a "C.R.M." together. I can feel a melt down in his expressions. He won't admit that the holidays mean something to him. I hang a few coloured bulbs up on his I.V. pole anyway. He's Muslim, I'm a Jew. Christmas! Why not?

There are three kids stuck in isolation for the holidays: Stella and Tin-tin and Diane, who is the only adolescent for miles. She is in the abyss of her imprisonment, deprived of her boyfriend, her little sister and most physical freedoms. We were told that her sister is a compatible donor for the B.M.T. and that it might save her life. To boost her morale, we do a "pas de deux" and then sing "Under the Boardwalk." Slowly but surely she relaxes and a smile reappears on her face. But wouldn't it be cool if the boyfriend, Nick could slip in next to her? That would be the best present.

We see that Stella is chatty and playful, she has gained confidence in herself. It feels like she uses us, like most little 5 year old girls use their dolls: to mother; to confide in; to scold; and, sometimes to abuse. The nurses claim that Stella still shuts down from time to time but that her voice has now been found.

At the end of the day, Nad leaves in a flurry, going home to her parents in the provinces for the holidays. It takes me two hours to get out the hospital; undressing and washing, taking my time to write up the day, cheer up the head nurse, say my Christmas wishes to one and all. It feels like I'd be spending the night. A silent night, a holy night.

34.

Swine Lake

The night before Christmas, I get an e-mail from Diane:
"Hello Girafe!!!

Hope that YOU are well. Sorry I haven't written for a while. Now let's get down to business: My sweetie pie came by and we were not well behaved at all. But don't worry, I didn't take any risks. Even though I'm in aphasia, my medication protects me from all the naughty germs. Am I a crrrrrrazy kid. OR WHAT?

I will be slugging it out here in isolation without my sister and dogs. I REALLY want to go home by New Year's eve to see my boy-friend. *padabooom padaboom*. I'm kind of sad right now!!! Fed up with this "cell" and being separated from "my love" for so long. I want to go home and have a normal life. My courage has dropped into my socks.

I should get my blood tests back soon to see if my white cell count has grown.

I'm impatiently waiting for your answer, Ms. Giraffe.

See ya,

D.

****

On Christmas day, Dr. Basket (Pierrette), "Catapoof" (her friend, Sylvie), "Foofool the Fairy-pest" (my daughter Lailah) and I go unannounced on holiday rounds to the hospital. It's our personal tradition. We do simple parades sprinkled with song and bubbles. We stop to see the kids stuck in bed, their families and the team of nurses on duty. No one expected to see us. In the nurse's lounge, there are scads of luxury chocolates and gourmet snacks to munch on between visiting rooms.

Imagine the ample Dr. Basket leading Louie's even rounder, mildly drunken uncle in a tragicomic dance of Swan Lake. All this takes place in front of Mimi's reception throne. The "lake" is created by pouring a cup of fountain water onto the floor. La Giraffe plays the flute to assure all symphonic effects while Foofool blows a myriad of bubbles and Catapoof poses, all arms up as an evergreen forest. The empty space transforms instantly into a "village square" with a colony of parents, children with IV poles, some in wheel chairs, and a crowd of nurses. The two "primavera ballerinas" enter from behind Mimi's desk and perform an improvised pas de deux. The grand finale has a flourish of tango steps and Basket, almost in the splits, tears her knickers. This produces "pee in your pants" laughter and wild applause from all as we disappear into the B.M.T. U. to continue our parade.

Once into our special gear, Dr. Dora tells us the best Christmas tale ever: "Last evening, the night nurse decided that she wants to surprise Martin by putting on a full Santa Claus outfit, which she had specially "sterilised' for the occasion. With a "Ho- Ho-Ho", white beard and boots, 'Santa' turned down the lights and snuck into his room with a pile of gifts. Even though his eyes were closed, she knew that he was wide-awake and thoroughly excited. Just for the record, he pretended to snore, but kept a slit of eyeball open. 'Santa' tiptoed to his bedside table, emitting another soft "Ho-Ho-Ho" as she put the presents down onto the bed table. Tin-tin did not budge. Later on, when the nurse had changed back into her uniform and went back to the room with some medication, she casually asked: "Did 'Santa' come down the chimney yet?" Martin took his habitual pause to ponder and thoughtfully replied: "You tink you twicked me but I don't tink Thanta uses the thame perfume as nurthes."

Our hearts full to the brim, Lailah and I go home to light our Chanukah candles while Pierrette and Sylvie drive north to a warm fireplace and holiday dinner.

Before sleeping I check my e-mail:

"Dear clownettes,

Merry Christmas You Rotten Potatoes! Burp! Schlurp, fart! from the two blue Elefants of Peking! Thanks for the surprise visit. Y'all are terrorist clowns.

Love from Diane and her 'favourite' nurse"

P.S. The docs say I can escape for New Years Eve and get a dose of romance-o-therapy."

35.

Tap dancing in a minefield

It's a week past the New Year and I can't shake the heaviness in my chest. Nadine calls me last night to announce two deaths: Elizabeth, the day after Christmas (we had expected her silk strand to break); and Momo. MOMO? ! I feel like I am in a free fall off a high cliff. MOMO? My certitudes are crushed. There's shattered glass in my heart. Damn. Damn. Damn. He was not supposed to go. Nadine says that no one knows what happened. The chemo was going well. He had a curable type of leukaemia. We all had imagined that he would heal with time. Who says that medicine is an exact science?

Gone: The ghetto teen; my big bad teddy bear from the land of pit bulls; who stole cars; who only read the driver's code; decked out in gold chains; always wearing his yellow sweat suit; splashing on his mystery citrus aftershave before a clown visit or a nurse would change an I.V. bag. I gave him such a hard time. Flirting my clown best. He rejected me with such finesse. We had begun to have good talks. About life, about cars, about girls. About nothing. I can still see Momo staring at the ceiling, at those moronic stars I placed there to watch over him. Gone. My last image: Momo placidly revelling in a gory Gladiator video, on Christmas day as my lovely daughter Lailah, Foofool the fairy, fluttered in the background. They were both so full of life in that moment.

It's gonna be hard to go back in a few days. A clown colleague once said: "Some days it feels like we're tap dancing in the mine fields."

36.

Syncopation

Mimi says, "There will be soft breezes after the hurricane."

The clowning day starts off weird and off centre. Nadine and I can't get into a clear rhythm. I go left, she turns right. I start to play music, she begins to talk. Giraffe sulks and she doesn't even notice. La Mouche dashes into each room, as I force myself to tag along and keep up with her pace. Exasperated and lost, I attempt to give her clown codes and fool's clues to communicate what I want, but it is to no avail. I feel like a moronic snail. Is it hypoglycaemia? Are we in mourning, in denial about the hard times? Or are we merely rushed, because we have started late? Nadine hates being late. I hate feeling incompetent. There are days of dissonance in a clown marriage, like in any relationship. It's important, not to get stuck. And we have a bad case of stuck'n'stubborn-itis.

Out of mere survival, I choose to do a solo parade around the ward for 15 minutes and finally take a breather. Finally La Mouche notices me and we agree to duck into a private corner for a talk. We need to clarify our feelings, untangle the string that connects our kite to the earth. La Giraffe to La Mouche. With both noses down, our words are softened by the deep respect we have for each other and our ability to communicate. Our history together is unforgettable: after all we had weathered the rocky roads of this leukaemia ward together, until now, always knowing when we needed a hot toddy and a good cry. This 10 minute pause was all that was required. Now, the rest of the day can flow and harmonise. We are still "married." We sing and dance again and I will even let La Mouche shut me in the closet or pour water over my head. I remember how much I love this clownette.

Stella is hidden in her silence again, maybe because her father has showed up. I would too if my father shows up after a 3 month absence. He is the discreet type, reading a mystery novel in his corner, not really paying attention to his daughter. She is in another world: distant, contemplative, un-playful. We can't force anything. The nurse reassures us and says, "Stella has now opened up to about 50% of the staff, and she has her favourites."

Diane is back for a week of "cocktails" and suddenly notices how tall her clownettes are. I guess she always observes us in the Cleopatra lounging position.

Martin is leaving his big B.M.T. bubble after 35 days. He looks lost and refuses to talk. We give him a silent demonstration of making fancy soap bubbles: a square one; a space ship; a merry go round; a caterpillar; and, the clincher, a belly dancer bubble head with boobs. Dr. Loon used to give me virtuoso bubble lessons back in the Bronx.

110

At the end of a long day Nad and I agree to go to the movies and dinner. Pure escapism! We also need some inclownito time together and probably a stiff drink.

37.

Dr. Josephine and already 70 "guests"

This morning in the hospital cafeteria at the "hour of the white coat", I muse while waiting for Stephie, Dr. Josephine. The place is swarming with doctors and interns, some looking at x -rays over coffee, a few just letting off steam after a strenuous night "on call" and some smelling of a shower and a warm croissant.

I flashback to when I am 12 and visiting my cherished grandma, "Poochee" in the Intensive Care Unit after she has had a massive heart-attack. My mom left me alone with her for twenty minutes while she rushed down to the cafeteria for a coffee. There are a dozen machines beep-beeping, toot-tooting and weird lights blinking. I was frozen with intimidation until Poochee opened her wrinkled eyes and started softly speaking to me about her Rumanian strudel recipe. Just like that. About to die and she talked about cooking. I began to hallucinate the taste of her pastries. It calmed my nerves to hear her. We were passionate about food and eating in my family. Cookbooks were read in our house like morning newspapers. For generations of wandering Jews, food and cooking had been a true remedy for coping with tragedy. Whenever I have had a hard day at the hospital, or even a mediocre one, I go to the market, pick out serendipitous ingredients and concoct a fabulous meal. Self soothing rituals. Poochee taught me that.

I'm still waiting for Steph. Maybe I need a second cup of coffee. Why do all hospitals have lousy coffee?

Another gush of images start to flow from 1968 when I was 18, taking pre-med classes and working as a nurse's aide in the physical therapy department at a Philadelphia Hospital. I can still smell the bleached uniform I was issued and remember how proud I was to be admitted into the healers club.

I always did my job, was on time, attentive to detail, but felt like a walking catastrophe; since I was not prepared for so much emotional attachment at the hospital, I cried my eyes out every night after work and managed to fall in love with two patients. The first, Jim, a young Irish cop, had been shot in the brain by a ghetto kid. The tragedy made all the headlines four months before. In the 60's, I was a long-haired, beaded hippie, political activist, and on principle, hated cops, but this man was a sleeping prince. My secret Celtic someone. Just my type. Who cared if he was policeman? Despite 120 days of immobility, he still had a gorgeous body (I am still a sucker for jocks. It's a long story.) I always spoke to Jim on the sly, while he was on a stretcher getting hydrotherapy. I could fill those tubs to the perfect temperature of 99 degrees Fahrenheit without a thermometer. Just a dip of an elbow and I knew. The treatments lasted 40 minutes and I was supposed to stay by his side, keeping the water temperature stable and massaging his hands. Nobody communicated with guys in comas in 1968. It wasn't done. People thought they were dead meat. Rumours had it that Jim's fiancée stopped coming to visit after one month and that she was going to marry someone else. In those 40 minutes, twice a week, I first told him who I was, what I was wearing (under my uniform), followed by the front-page news. Then I'd share some lame stories about my disastrous love life and caress his limp, yet elegant hands. Hoping. Imagining that those long-lashed eyes would open up to look at me. Just once, to let me know that he had heard everything and that my conversations mattered. After all, his breathing pattern would change each time I spoke to him. Wasn't that a sign of listening, of life? Years later, when I clowned for my first patient in a coma, I felt that I could talk to her and that she was somehow listening.

The U.S.A. was in the throes of the Vietnamese war and three kids with severe napalm burns had been sent to Philly for hydrotherapy, skin grafts and adoption. Besides going to get my boys in their rooms, then zig zag them down the halls in their wheel chairs, my job was to peel all the bandages off their mutilated bodies and lower them naked into a soothing pool of medicated water. I had to be careful and slow. Their raw wounds smelled terrible and I was so embarrassed taking their clothes off. As I tried not to look or hurt them, we often laughed hard. Pain remedies were not used for these procedures nor were they "fashionable" with the doctors yet. My favourite boy was the lanky Tuan. He was 17 and from Saigon. We didn't have much in common other than the fact that he had gone to a French high school and that I was a confirmed Francophile with a 200 word vocabulary. We had a mad but silent crush on each other. It was a beginning. "Bone-jour Tuan."

Since the age of four, I wanted to be a real doctor like my grandfather, Morris and now, not to disappoint my father who spent so much money for my schooling. Or my mom, who had wanted to be a doctor too, but had four brats instead. Yet, now I knew that it would never happen. The stress and the grief during those three months in Philadelphia poisoned my dreams. All those competitive doctors pitted against nurses. Nurses speaking down to aides. Aides treating my sleeping prince like a package of flesh. I was sick and tired of crying every night, miserable, fed up with the medical profession and only happy when I was fooling around with the patients. Fooling around wasn't a profession, was it? I felt like a failure. A cop out. A ninny. A clown? I went straight back to college, dropped all my pre-med classes and signed up for the theatre department. It was a curious decision since I was basically shy. At the end of the school year, my drama professor suggested that I go to the Barnum and Bailey clown school in Florida. Huh? At the time I felt insulted. Didn't I have the talent to play Lady Macbeth?

***

There is a surprise metro strike and my partner has just walked miles to the hospital. Stephie, Dr. Josephine, 15 years my junior, is a high-energy clownette and gives this old dog a breakneck run in the park. Our clown marriage is based upon sibling rivalry. We call ourselves "The Spit Sisters." My own memories of squabbling with my brothers and sister inspire plenty of material to nourish our improvisations. We juggle sisterly love and conflict with enthusiasm and are hungry to play.

The place is full of children after the holiday drought. In the locker room I take ten minutes to leaf through our journal and count 70 separate cases "seen by clowns" since we have started the program in the fall. Why did Mimi say that the "sun was shining brightly" when I know there is a black cloud lurking?

The thunderhead appears in Ophelia's room. During the nurse's report, we learn that the child's mom died of a stroke on Christmas day. When it rains it floods in her life. Having shared so many tender moments with Ophelia since September, it feels obscene to carry on clown business as usual. I can't face her as if nothing has changed. I am compelled to make a visit. Just the two of us, our two hearts and our four eyes. Nose up or nose down? Stop over in my civvies, before getting in costume or go as my clown? I don't want to transgress my role with her, nor do I want to infringe upon her mourning. It is clear, she has always known me as Giraffe. Not as Caroline. So there is no need to torture myself. La Giraffe can handle the situation. After putting on my red-nose, costume and ears, I strand Dr. Josephine to dillydally with Stella who has just been released from the B.M.T.U. . (Did her B.M.T. work?)

Simplicity rules in a complex situation. Ophelia is alone and concentrating on a picture book. I tip-toe to her side and whisper into her ear, "I have heard about your mamma this morning and I'm sorry. I want you to know that, that I am sorry." Immediately Ophelia sighs and says: "Merci, Gigi." She seems relieved. Me: "Do you still want clowns today?" To which she replies: "Mais, oui." No more, no less.

Knock-knock! In trots Dr. Josephine with our trusty assistant, Miss Stella and within 30 seconds, the two little girls and two big clownettes are having a duck and lamb sing along. Every tune we come up with has to be sung with Baaaaaaaa or Quaaaack. It puts balm on our hearts to see Ophelia playing with Stella and the two of them giggling together.

Although Stella is fine about baaaa-ing and quack-ing, she has lost her speaking tongue again. She hasn't lost her dancing feet. I think she is testing us, trying to see if we will try to squeeze words or coax phrases out of her. So we dance the rumba, tango, and the cha-cha-cha. We can wait, she'll talk when she's ready. In the meantime, we get a decent conga line happening down one length of the hallway with two nurses, one med student, three kids and four parents. By the time we get to the far window,

114

Stella's dainty legs are shaking so hard she has to go back to bed. These are the moments when you realise just how sick and weak the children are.

Put on the brakes! Ben's just arrived in an ambulance and is already in a diminuendo behind drawn curtains in a dark room. It's impossible to make contact with either mother or child. I feel the soft breeze of small wings trying to flap. Please stay alive kid. I'm getting a knot in my stomach from the perpetual roller coaster ride here. There have been enough strong emotions today.

Comic relief comes when the "spit sisters" invent a new game for Tin-tin. We encourage him to throw imaginary punches at us that send our bodies splattering onto the walls like bugs on windshields. He really can't get enough of this game and keeps yelling: "Encore, encore! I want to nail you to the walls!" It permits him, from a lying position, to play a hard-nosed, macho-boy, without really hurting a fly. Over and over we endure his imaginary punches and die a million deaths for his pleasure. Sometimes it must be a drag being everybody's "little treasure." Fighting with clowns is more fun and possibly useful.

38.

"I want my clowns right now!"

Mimi says: "the weather is calm, not boring with a few pink clouds gathering on the horizon." I ask if that means the Professor is out of town again. She winks and welcomes Dr. Bob and his hairy legs.

We have two charming new patients, Antoine (14 years old) and Alice (9 years old). We are immediately drawn to them. "I like them too much already." Back in my Bronx days, Dr. Meatloaf and I used to say this little phrase to keep a close check on keeping the right distance and getting over-attached to a kid. If you don't put 100% of your clown heart and talent to the service of a patient, you cannot do first class work. The risk is always worth taking. The process is more important than the results. But it takes lucidity, frequent self-evaluation, communicating with your partner and sometimes a good cry.

Alice has jumped the gate and was recently initiated into "the world of illness" with a two week parentheses in the I.C.U.3. Leukaemia is often treated as an emergency. Thus we inherit a new treasure. Mom on one side of the bed, grandma on the other, looking like kind-hearted bookends for one jewel of a mute princess. Since Alice had endured a tracheotomy4 with an incubation, as a result has not yet recovered an ability to speak. She is clearly, still in pain. Her immense china-blue eyes, set in a porcelain-white face speak volumes and honey-coloured hair flow onto her shoulders. After a romantico-goofy rap and flute extravaganza, the princess bestows a most luminous smile upon us and we float away to the next.

Antoine has a tangled jungle of I.V. lines going in and out of each arm, a swollen knee and more than his share of pain. He is described by the staff as: "first in his class and a champion athlete. He is handsome, shy and adores rap music. (A job for Bob.) His dad plays the bagpipes and that embarrasses him to death." He's signed up for a steep medical hike here.

Martin's about to leave for a rehab centre, but still does not want to walk or get out of bed. We stage a life and death battle between our puppets, Lili, the fearless farting mouse and CooCoo the cowardly, cussing parrot for him. The mouse and bird beg to leave the hospital with him for a change of scenery.

Dr. Bob and I are a raucous duo, always fighting and singing loudly. Stella welcomes us into her room (back in isolation) with: "I want my clowns now!" for she's decided to talk again! The clowning is launched with a thunderous Giraffe sneeze into Bob's cap. He scoops the imaginary snot out of his cap and we play with the make believe balls that can fly and bounce around the room. They grow from ping pong to balloon size and we throw them as at each other, onto the four walls and then at Stella. It's innocent fun, rhythmed by repetitive sneezing, schlurping and wild boomerang effects.

In the middle of a new ahhh-chooo, Stella shouts out: "Watch out! La Giraffe wants to throw up." When any child tosses in a new idea during an improvisation, it's our absolute duty to act on it immediately. Clowns always say YES. So, here I am with two fingers pinching my lips, puffed out cheeks and ready to spout imaginary vomit. Bob responds by opening a drawer for me to barf into. Mom and Stella scream: "No!" So I go for Mom's purse. "Noooo!" they yell. The closet? "No, no, noooooooo!" Then I bolt into the hallway, to "retch" out of sight. The nurse on duty gives me one of those looks that stops me in my tracks. She comments on the coincidence that Stella happens to have a real vomiting reflex, which is a mystery to one and all. Bad smells, new medications, many things can provoke extreme nausea. I was the same at her age. Still am. The nurse is intrigued by the whole scene. Sometimes in our choice of play we unconsciously "pick up" on something like this. It is important to act on one's instincts without over interpreting the results. Children need to play with what's around. Body fluids are onmi-present.

I can hear a cascade of laughter coming out of the room, so I go in for more action! We exhaust this theme and made a date with Stella for more exciting "body function" games next week. Farting, burping and "pee pee-ca ca" games are popular with most younger hospitalised kids. Beats juggling or magic. Later on that same nurse tells us that Stella's vomiting "habit" has calmed down and has almost disappeared.

A day with Coco-a-Gogo

I take a "break" and have decided to spend the next two weeks in the General Paediatrics ward. With my partner of the day, Helen, Coco-a-Gogo, we make the rounds to the infant, small children and adolescent wards as well as the emergency room. In one day we visit diabetics, a few sickle-cell pain-crisis babes, asthmatics in for a first hospitalisation, a few teenagers who have made suicide attempts, a bouquet of infants with stomach flu and severe dehydration and the classic winter bronchitis infant crowd. The emergency room is packed with over-heated toddlers, two kids with broken arms, three asthma attacks and a sprinkling of stressed out multi-ethnic parents. It's clear, I welcome the change of pace from the leukaemia planet with it's overflowing rivers of tragedy.

I adore the way the village fool can wander in this particular building. Two clownette nomads running up and down the stairs, going from the day clinic to the baby ward and the teen ward. Then with a lovely "parade" in the underground hallways we arrive in the emergency room at the end of our day's roving.

Coco-a-Gogo is a miniature disjointed meteorite of ongoing creativity and red-nosed locomotion. Working with her helps me learn about counterpoint and suspension, stillness and activity. Her imagination defies gravity and leaves me humble. I admire Helene's mastery of our work. The day's rhythm was extravagant. Going from the softness of fluted lullabies to a two-headed, Jerry Lewis-like monster struggling to untangle its limbs.

At the end of the teen hallway, Samantha, 16, is waiting in her bed. We've known her for three years on and off. She is in the final stages of Cystic Fibrosis. A frail mermaid who's every breath is a heroic effort. Despite everything, it is stunning to see how quickly Samantha clicks into clown mode, how the slightest clown noise will trigger play. Here's this milk-skinned girl closing her eyes to concentrate on producing strange "animal" sounds to make us laugh and she can barely inhale. We dialogue with her as hiccuping seals, farting gremlins, crazed Martians and burping frogs for a solid ten minutes. Before Coco-a-Gogo and I float through the "red curtain", we play a flute duet of Fellini-esque waltzes as Samantha lets her transparent eyelids lower, and sinks into a dream.

La Giraffe spinning is by the end of the day, dizzy with fatigue. Another clown's words of wisdom whispers in my mind: "Sometimes the great memories are as difficult to let go of, as the tragedies."

Tonight Nadine calls to say that she and Loulou, that traitor, got married with Stella's complicity. There will be revenge! Marriage, divorce, intrigue, murder, war. This is all part of the Big Clown Soap

Opera. They are running themes and stories that we develop with children who are hospitalised long term. These themes and stories are laced with a palette of primary emotions that can be expressed purely or may be combined as a mixture of two or three underlying feelings. For example, bravery can be born of anger and fear, and through the play with the clowns, it can transform into immense jubilation. It's important to keep strong emotions fluid and moving.

A professional clown is trained to use a range of emotions, with text or improvisation as one of the basic tools of his work. These emotions can be played out in a wide range of "scenes", with the clowns and the children acting as performers or as directors. The clowns can go far on this theatrical voyage with the child, as long as he respects the limits that the child gives him. What is important is that no one gets stuck too long in one strong emotional state.

Clowns give priority to facial expression and body language which are often more revealing and more truthful than verbal expression. In some cases the use of a puppet or music can facilitate this process, by taking a theatrical situation as far as the child wants to explore it even when he is at the risky boundary between fantasy and an intense reality. However, the clown must take care that these scenes stay within the realm of theatrical play and that it never becomes too concrete, even when reality is extremely close to the fantasy.

Here are a few examples of emotions and their corresponding clown play:

FEAR (worry, fright, embarrassment, apprehensiveness, nervousness, shyness, terror) corresponding to: imitating monsters; performing horror shows; playing tricks on staff; creating fake medical procedures; doing magic; and, hiding somewhere in the child's room.

SADNESS (despair, nostalgia, self-pity, melancholy, concern, grief, humiliation) corresponding to: tragic love scenes; tender lullabies, loss of a prop and, the clown as a victim, crying because he is lonely or left out.

ANGER (rage, jealousy, outrage, defiance, recklessness, contemptuousness, meanness) corresponding to: thievery; fights; shooting guns; wild dancing; clumsiness with the body and with objects such as doors that won't open, tripping and bumping into imaginary obstacles.

JOY (happiness, love, playfulness, flirting, enthusiasm, hilarity, silliness, inspiration, tenderness) corresponding to: clown marriages; imaginary celebrations; parades; treasure hunts; wild goose chases; and, water fights.

40.

Rituals

I'm still in The General Paeds ward this week, giddy knowing I will spend more time away from leukaemia and playing with an old favourite team of nurses and doctors. They are a wacky and loveable group with whom the clowns have developed dozens of rituals and running jokes. The furlough from haematology continues.

When you plant a garden, you must continue to water the flowers. So, in order to maintain a healthy hospital marriage that is full of fun and a tad sexy while preserving a serious spirit of "health care", one of the golden threads that we weave into hospital daily life is a large number of running jokes. These personalised customs bring unity to the hospital village by creating kooky rituals that have nothing to do with hierarchy, medical business or power. These little routines are absurd, non-direct and create metaphors that encourage another way of thinking. Often they jolt a staff member out of his "reality", catching everyone off guard and in some odd way preparing us all for a real "emergency."

Each clown in L.R.M. has his own book of recipes. Professor Leonie in Nantes greets one and all by raising her arms to the sky and sighing: "it's allll rrrrright!" In the haematology ward, the day cannot begin without asking Mimi for the "weather report." In the adolescent ward Dr Chips and I started a tradition of hanging up clown laundry (rubber fish, polka dotted under garments, doll clothes) on one floor and checking back several times a day to see if it is "dry." Dr. Babycakes likes to put clothespins on the bottom of nurses uniforms without anyone noticing until later when he counts how many he has "tagged." In the hallways of haematology, when we shout, "It's a hold up!" the arms of a group of medical students automatically go up, as a clown will try a quick tickle on some unsuspecting ribs. La Giraffe is obsessed with checking the height of a doorway before going under to make sure that she won't bump her head and the kids are quite professional about reassuring her. In the B.M.T.U., another Babycakes speciality is to create the illusion of a deep hole in front of a patient's window. He "falls" down when he reaches this magical spot and does a splendid pantomime of "walking up the stairs" afterwards. He has even gotten the nurses to maintain this visual gag when the clowns are not there. One Professor keeps the collar of his white coat in a chic upwards position. When an innocent batch of new med students arrive we fast talk them into believing that it is the only "cool" way to dress in our ward. Then they all walk around with collars up, looking stupid.; I adore creating jokes with the nurses about the varying degrees of their "burnout" calling it: "barbecue; shish ka bob; hamburger; and toast. Are you fried today or just scorched?"

Dr. Ida, the head of the department has been known to imitate a rooster better than any clown in L.R.M. . When Dr. Balthazar arrives on her ward he always pretends that she is the "landlady" and that he is late on paying the rent. They squawk and scream from one end of the hallway to the other. When Coco-a-Gogo starts to bark in the hallways, Dr. Ida always lets out a few raucous crows and then yells from her office: "Dogs are not allowed in the teen ward!" All this happens while patients, med students and parents look on boggled yet happy to discover another side of the good doctor's personality. As for Dr. N., chief resident, she once borrowed Dr. Babycakes oversized clown shoes for making her medical rounds, doing a soft-shoe dance in each patient's room. It was her secret fantasy and Dr. Ida approved. They are a splendid team of healers and collaborators.

I partner today with the Scottish, tap-dancing wonder, Margo, Dr. Pigtails. Together we are a four-legged festival of musical comedy routines. We share a love for singing American, Irish and Scottish songs and making spicy side -remarks in our mother tongue.

We pop into Samantha's room to check her out. Her mom and an unidentified woman are plopped in chairs hovering near the bed. Samantha and her breathing struggles are noticeably improved from Monday. With others around, her behaviour is conventional and the clown trigger doesn't work. We have normal human conversations. It's a pity when you know her potential for goofiness. I guess she wants to keep us to herself, without witnesses to our secret games. Yet, this uncanny ability of hers to become silly and fly off the deep end is just under the surface. I've rarely seen anything quite like it.

Other clowns in the company who know and visit Samantha feel that each time they see her might well be the last time. Just now, Margo and I avoid exchanging our emotions, but with one look into her eyes, I know we are feeling the same dread. We are not in denial, we just need to get through the day without bursting into tears.

One thing's for sure. You cannot perform for a child who is facing eternity if you have not had the courtesy to fantasise once or twice (a year?) about your own death. It's as scary as hell, but you must force yourself to imagine what it might feel like when you are short of breath, weaker than Tinkerbell's shadow and facing a separate world; one without your mother, dark chocolate or birds. I'm not joking. It's not fun but, I make myself do it again and again, and rarely speak about it. I feel almost ashamed confessing it. I am always alone (can't imagine who wants to share this one), usually in bed before going to sleep (feels less distracting and safer) and when I'm in a fairly positive mood (am not the suicidal type). Usually after a few minutes of swallowing panic, I begin to calm down, feel less "threatened" and understand that it is not death that scares me, but dying. In fact, I am 300% alive until my hearts stops, I no longer breathe or have brain activity and no matter what I do or think about it all,

I better just stay "in the moment", help my fellow mammals any way I can and enjoy every bloody second I get until the clock stops. There goes another taboo down my clown drain.

We slide into the room of a 12 year old boy with multiple handicaps. He is lying on his side, facing the window, eyes wide, his features all scrunched. In a blink, Miss Pigtails and I simultaneously start a four song medley: "Stormy Weather"; the theme song from "Hair" ("When the moon is in the second sun, and Jupiter aligns with Mars"); then "Where have all the flowers gone", that Joan Baez classic; and, "Good Night Sweetheart, it's time to go-oh...." (a doo-wop standard). Our harmonies are flawless and our timing feels cosmic. We get a mad case of the giggles. The miracle of the perfect partner at the perfect moment happens again. It's a case of mutual delight. As the boy's eyes brighten and focus, a peaceful look invades his face. His body relaxes. He listens with such concentration, I can imagine his thoughts dancing with the curtains. We ski out on a grace note and a flourish, holding pinkies like first graders.

Right afterward in the intimacy of the teen T.V. lounge, we find ourselves surrounded by three kids: an 8 year old Algerian girl with a fresh case of diabetes; a depressed blond, draped over one of the ratty couches; and, a black- eyed beauty plopped on her side. We were told in the morning that two of the girls were victims of severe physical and sexual abuse. Inspiration comes as my flute takes off almost without me and Dr. Pigtails starts to undulate and wiggle around for the kids. I feel like a reincarnated snake charmer and Pigtails reveals her talent for belly dancing. High-pitched giggling starts to bubble up from the girls and floods the room. The black-eyed sultana comes to life and instigates an oriental dance that blows us all away. She closes her eyes and performs for five solid minutes. The other two girls clap in rhythm and seem to forget the time of day and their many troubles. Our young dancer feels safe in the company of other women and lets the room fill with her sensuality and a deep-seated pride in her virtuosity. As her dance ends, I nearly burst into tears and we all break into unbridled yoo yoo's.

For a brief time, here are five odd sisters, suspended on a planet, protected and united. Is this a moment when some healing can occur? Would it last after we go? Margo and I leave the room feeling part of each other's and the girls' lives. Change can take place; even by increments. I cannot bear knowing what has happened to these girls, so that they must spend the next three weeks in the hospital. Once again I need a double dose of denial to get through the day, be a good enough partner for Pigtails and to stay true to La Giraffe. We have shared something exceptional, private and maybe sacred.

41.

"Y'all should entertain in a zoo!"

I am home, back to the haematology ward and it's the big bad flu season. Even children with leukaemia get it, nurses with immunity get it and my Nadine is shaky, coughing like a seal. She will have to wear two surgical masks all day to protect the children from her germs. Mimi says: "Things are calm, relatively speaking."

During the nurse's report, a vision appears on the other side of the glass door of Miss Stella, our cherished ex-mute, pacing the hallways like a famished tiger waiting to pounce on her clowns. The big news is in remission and after one more month in France can fly back to her far-away island of flowers. Cured? After we don our noses, she follows us into every room that doesn't require a mask and participates in all of our improvisations. A nurse, tearing out of the day clinic after performing a L.P., arms full of blood samples, stops to look at the 3 of us and declares: "All I do today is make little children cry" (why is she so hard on herself?) and then, she puts the pause button on, smiles and continues: "That Stella has blossomed, thanks to you clowns." Soul Balm for us!

Karen, our rather proper teen who had lost all of her hair on her last birthday, is here for a monthly chemo. She's wearing a slick, black wig, Cleopatra style. Wasn't she a blond? The most surprising event takes place as we are leaving her room. Stella's eyes get big and round as Karen starts to pout like a jilted five year old, saying:" You need to spend more time with me. Will you clowns visit during my upcoming B.M.T., it's going to be so long and boring and would you teach me to sing? I want to start now?" EUREKA! Since Karen's always been the grin and bear it type, this is a huge step forward for her - to be demanding. With Stella's help on the pickle-squeaker, La Mouche and I work Karen into an improvised doo-wop. I don't dare look into her eyes while we are singing, for fear that she will clam up, feeling judged. Sure enough, a voice emerges and weaves itself into our ta doo ta da's, like she has always known how to sing and improvise. These unexpected, pocket-sized wonders mean that for the two-month lockup in the B.M.T.U., we have a built-in tool for sharing creativity with her. You need resources in that coop.

Diane is stable; chatty. La Mouche and I play at being fashion models, using everything in sight (paper towels, masks, plastic booties) for making hats and dresses. Before leaving, she said she wrote a new e-mail. I'll read it when I get home.

Melancholy has put a sombre veil on Martin who lies barely moving and not in good enough shape to leave the ward yet. He's fed up, yet stoic. Persuading him that he will soon need big-brother skills, we

124

persuade Tin-tin to diaper a doll, give it a bottle of milk and then we all sing his favourite lullaby before departing. That gets him going a bit. "Viens mon petit ours, dans mes bras, la nuit est tombé et j'ai un peu froid..." As Dr. Basket often says: "This kid just needs a good dose of clown."

You never know when you step through a door what might happen in a room. Polite kids can turn into impish devils with just a little bit of prodding and sometimes the wild ones show a need for a moment of saintly silence. Alice borders on the angelic so we provoke a collective ode to the female chest! It is a girly-girly moment. Just for us silly females. Her mom comes out with some winners: "Mandarins, clementines, melons, boobies, air bags, bazookas." Alice and Stella double over with laughter as we go from the poetic to the goofy. La Mouche threatens all our chests with the squeaker.

We try in vain to make contact with Louie. A move to the B.M.T.U. has seriously affected him. He ignores us, persists in staring at the laptop computer and playing his ritual games with Lara Croft. This may be the only thing that can ground him right now. He knows just how patient we are, but each time we announce our departure, Lou pipes up saying: "But, I just won again." or "Hey clowns, I'm now at level five!" We can't find the key to anything else; it might stay this way for a while and it's frustrating. Next time Nad and I promise ourselves that we will try a non-verbal approach. Sigh. This little soldier is in the middle of a sterile white battlefield. We retreat.

When we are leaving a 12 year old boy's room (still in the B.MT.U.), I notice an empty, slightly bloody I.V. bag scotch-taped to the wall. It has been used for his bone marrow transplant. It hangs like an other worldly oil portrait of a loved elder or an eerie trophy reminding him of his body's battles with fate. We do not know what to make of it so I ask a male nurse why some of the kids keep their bone marrow bags pinned on the wall. He says: "It is just a souvenir of the person that gave them the gift of life. It's like a heart transplant patient who keeps a small box of their donor's ashes." This is all a bit morbid for us. We forget how much the medical staff needs "gallows humour" to survive. It's a well-kept secret.

As we write up our journal, we hear Stella chirping and prancing from room to room. Maybe she is excited about leaving for the islands soon. I can actually imagine the kid becoming a clown-doctor one day, repairing the souls of other children like herself. I remember another girl, a bit older who also went home, and who carried on our work in her own special way. Her name was Isabella and she lived in the oncology ward for way too long. She slept far too much for the good doctors' taste but kids do that when they have brain tumours. She had a sign on her door that said, "Only clowns can wake me up." And we did often. One day the doctors told her parents that it would be better if she return home, to their island in Spain, that they were out of cures. Isabella told her parents: "I'm NOT going back there unless there are clowns." So, her parents searched every corner of their land for "red-noses" and could only find a street performer, a nursery school teacher and an ageing circus clown. Isabella, who was only 11 years old became their clown-doctor master. After all, she had first-hand experience in France. This was how "La Medica Sonrisa" was born, the first clown-doctors in Majorca. For a year Isabella "trained" them right from her hospital bed and then flew away one sad day with the teaching manual. That is a kid who still keeps the angels laughing.

***

I get home, turn on my laptop and check for e-mail from Diane.
"Dear Giraffe,
This is a petite coo-coo from little old me to prove that my computer is working perfectly well. I'm still locked up in the old bubble. I had a super day, although I'm wiped from the chemo, even saw some people I actually adore. Now, I'm gonna have a good night. Thanks for writing back. I LOVE getting e-mail. It certainly took awhile to get it working. Sorry if I'm not so quick on the response end. See you idiots soon. And now a word from my favourite nurse: Yo, G-raf. If you are reading this at your so-called desk, stop pretending that you are working... We miss you, La Mouche too....Dr. Josephine, Dr. Chic, Basket, Dr. Bob and his hairy legs too. Sweet dreams and see you soon.
Kisses,
Diane and Nurse Honey-Bee
I discover that our clever little cheerleader sent a second message that must have been written after our elegant fashion show:
"Yo you two dimwits,
Your skit with La Mouche was 200% retarded, but what ever makes *you* happy.....makes *me* laugh. You are more like FLOP models than TOP models. Stick to zoo shows ladies and flyswatters on the bum for you, Mizz Mouche. So get a grip ladies and come up with some new material! In any case, I prefer gossip about love, romance, amour and hunks. Get the picture?
Hee-haw,
Diane"

42.

Pierrette, alias Dr Basket

Working with adolescents is like walking a highwire between self-doubt and fear of failure. It can put me into an emotional spin. My daughter, Lailah, now just over 20 years old, always shared just enough of her adolescent life, so that I was familiar with the current trends in slang, dress codes, academic tumult, music and romantic slaloms. This intimate knowledge of the teen world is a secret weapon, but also is my Achilles heel. Once in a moment of anger my daughter, then 15 years old, yelled at me: "You might spend your time making other kids laugh, but I do not find you funny at all. And if I am ever sick don't you dare send in those tasteless clowns!" This turned out to be a vital clue to approaching hospitalised adolescents.

The best advice you can give when working with adolescents is not to enter into either a seductive or a conflictual mode of expression with them. They will give you the keys, if you listen. Then doors open and you can communicate. The more I have accepted just how nerdy my Giraffe character is, the funnier the teens find me. But when I get attached to a particular adolescent, my sense of professional distance is not always as clear, or as healthy as it should be. When you reach this point (of no return), ruled by sentiment, you must let your partner dominate and sometimes take over the clown relationship. Otherwise, falling from that high emotional cloud when you are not ready, (you never are) is damaging. I have consciously let myself get burned. We all do once or twice when the flames are so beautiful. It's about feeling your own threshold for suffering. Dr. Stubs, my boss in the States always gave this wise piece of advice to clown-doctors: "Pain is a given, suffering is a choice."

*

Pierrette, Dr. Basket is here today. It's been too long since we were partners.

Love is smiling tenderly on our two adolescents. Coming to Karen's door, looking through the window, we notice her face is glowing. Blissful lashes fluttering. Our eyes travel down her body to discover a young man, cross-legged on the foot of the bed, massaging two enraptured feet! It's not a good moment for two buffoons to bash in for a tacky joke-a-thon! Seeing our 2 mouths agape, Karen winks, sticks out a pink tongue and we exit.

Diane too, has a male visitor. After he leaves, she is a pink-cheeked, dreamy naiad all afternoon, soaking in the pleasure of her emotions. I swear I can see the walls in her room blushing for hours. We let her sit on a cloud of thump-thump-thump, before finally making our visit.

Ever since we've known Diane, she has been brilliant at keeping her spirits high and her imagination spiked with interest in red-hot romance intrigues. It never matters to any of us whether truth prevails. A made-up memory is as important as a true one when you are stuck in the B.M.T.U. for 2 months. We never talk about the "truth." Who cares? What counts is the flush and flow of sentiments that warm your blood and give your heart an after-glow for days. It's about building a secret garden. I have spent many hours with Diane recounting throbbing stories that I have read or heard about as well as digging up my old infatuations, embellishing them, clownifying them and then serving them up to her hungry ears.

All the chatter about horses and hip-hop takes a back seat to Diane's latest adventure but clowns can also be shy and respectful so the dialogue moves lickety-split from a few words about passion to the ever-loving animal theme. Diane promises: "When I become a veterinarian, which might take 7 more years, I will treat La Giraffe for free. Too bad for you, Basket you're not an animal." She has never spoken or even alluded to the future in our presence. We always just "stay in the moment", surfing reality. That is all an honest clown can do. So, to our surprise and in a tactful way, Diane shines a ray of hope into her future and, perhaps my own. Once in a while I have teased the kids by saying: "One day I'll be old, sick and in a hospital bed. Maybe you'll be my doctor." Diane would be the best healer. Creativity makes life worthwhile; humour gives hope, but doesn't love make life worth living?

From afar, I sight a white cotton beanie on Alice's head and this is how we know that she has lost her honey locks overnight. Usually the first chemo treatment does not cause hair loss. That would be too brutal. It conveniently happens with the second one and by then a kid has seen plenty of other bald kids and hopefully has adjusted to the idea of the eventual moulting.

She proudly presents her "Granny - V.D.O." today. She got this nickname because she brings a new movie cassette each day for Alice to watch. On today's menu: "Patch Adams"! Of all things. Alice still behaves too politely and she's too accommodating to everyone, forever compliant. Her Mona Lisa grin worries me. We have our work cut out for us. A polite child can be more difficult to reach than a belligerent teen. In contrast I remember an eight year-old boy with 3 quiet brothers sitting at his side. While we were "playing attention" to the brothers, he yelled: "Hey what about ME? I'm the one who's sick!"

Stella's broviac has been removed and although she is leaving "forever", returning to her sun-drenched country and adored siblings, I have never seen the little one so forlorn. She has gone limp with sadness.

Reanimating her smile was all that Dr. Basket and I were capable of doing.

There must be an uncanny, yet comfortable feeling when you are severely ill as a child. Once you adapt to the initial shock, learn to cope with the pain and the transformation of your body, as most kids do, you realise that you are loved by many people. Doctors, nurses, parents and even clowns comfort you and take care of you in so many ways. I can understand that the loss of this cocoon must count as a major moment when a child leaves the hospital "for good", cured. Being normal again is not so much fun. When you have lived through a trauma your survivor's medals and scars don't show on the surface. You have been the centre of so many people's preoccupations and now you sink back into the masses. You are no longer special and the loss of the "in danger of death" status must be terrifying, especially because everyone keeps saying how great it is that you can leave the hospital, that you are better!

Martin too, is finally shipping off but to rehab for more rest and recuperation. Tin-tin's mom has her hands full with the new-born baby plus two other ankle-biters and cannot take him back home yet. He is such an endearing blimp. His small body has blown out of proportion from high blood pressure, months of cortisone treatments and over eating. We coax him to a teetering vertical position with nursing assistance and we manage to create a musical farewell, parading around the hallways - a merry troop of fools making too much noise. The poor Bambino is out of breath after the first round and has to get back to a horizontal position. A special ambulance will fetch him later on. I'm going to miss my Tin-tin bird. And my mute fairy-sprite.

43.

I'm back

I leave town for two weeks of business trips for Le Rire Medecin and upon my return I make a R.D.V. with Nadine in a café to get the news. Despite the clouds of cigarette smoke, it's always comforting to wait for a dear friend in a Parisian bistro over a steaming espresso. The coffee machines are singing today. Nad finally arrives and plops down across from me offering one of her ear-to-ear smiles. "Ca va?"... "Ca va." It only takes four simple words for my Giraffe ears to open wide. I can already tell that in the last 15 days the news has not been catastrophic.

With her deep voice Nad starts: "Ophelia is sinking into a lake of conventional courtesy. She's present, yet not really here, seems happy to play simple games and sing yet won't show much feeling. Given her situation (of mourning), we didn't push too many buttons. Her granny sits guard. "She pauses and then continues: "Louie is still in the B.M.T.U. Business as usual, he starts off by hiding under the covers, tries some clown abuse to no avail, but when he hears 'Granny-Fart' joking with the clowns about recipes for apple pie, he emerges. Obviously wanting attention." "Naturally."

"Still there is something new in his behaviour. So guess what happens next? He takes out a book. Then he starts reading fairy tales for the "children" and that includes the noble Granny. Then Pina, Dr. Freida, who has never met him before, exclaims: 'He's so sweeeeeeet.' Can you believe it? There is someone who finds our Louie, the fearless outlaw killer! Sweet?"

We have a good laugh. If anyone ever asked me to define Louie, the terror is one word, "sweet" would not come to mind! Nevertheless, once we calm down we try to analyse this new element in the little guy's behaviour. We agree that even if his decision to tell fairy tales is incongruous with previous conduct it does help him take refuge and draw comfort in his imagination. The line between Lara Croft and a fairy is rather thin. Maybe next time we see him we should don long sparkling gowns, blond wigs and carry magic wands?

O.K. Nadine interjects, I'll be Tinker bell and you can be Glinda! Sweet Nad, she always know how to make me laugh.

In some hospitals, there is too much activity for the kids however this activity does not compensate for illness or for our adult guilt. [Children need fairy tales and fantasy images, which provide structures in a language they understand, to help them work though their own trials.] Their fantasy life is an essential outlet, a release from the day to day traumatic realities of their hospitalisation.]

132

Clowns don't have a copyright on fantasy and imagination. All professionals working with hospitalised children must be open to the images that these children provide, for the child often chooses a story that acts as a healing metaphor for them (for example Maurice's image of himself as the wind and Louie's fascination with "Tomb Raiders" and its heroine "Lara Croft"). These healing metaphors build resources for the child.

However because fantasy and imagination are some of the clown-doctor's basic 'tools', their work can sometimes be interpreted by healthcare workers in a superficial way. Because a hospitalised child laughs with the clowns, it does not mean that he is doing well psychologically or medically. When a child chooses to refuse interaction or cannot react positively to the clowns, it does not mean that he is depressed or has cut himself off from communicating with the world. Sometimes he needs to be alone or have a non-stimulating pause or engage in fantasy play on his own.

44.

The gift of life

Mimi gives us the weather report: "Blue skies, cool winds and the birds are chirping." The birds on today's menu are Coco-a-Gogo and La Giraffe.

Dr. Sam, our male intern apparently has "found" and adopted my mouse finger puppet. (I hadn't even noticed it was lost.) She must have escaped from my pocket last week. Mimi tells me that Sam has been having a jolly old time spooking the nurses and inching the furry creature into his daily doctor rounds, when he examines the kids. I wonder if he's scaring mouse-a-phobic moms, like I do? When I go to the lounge and confront him with the evidence, there is no way that he will surrender that mouse. So we agree that it is a permanent loan. He is becoming such a well-trained doctor.

My 9 year old "Uncle Jack" is just in the day clinic for his yearly check up. I have known him for over five years since he was four and was first being treated for a tumour near his left ear. I convinced him to adopt La Giraffe during one of our improvisations. This is a role-reversal game and a slick trick to create closeness with some kids. When I asked to be adopted, Jack chose to be my uncle, not my grandmother, not my big brother. From then on, each time we saw each other, I got the full treatment: scolded for not washing my ears properly; reprimanded for not doing my homework; punished for spilling water all over my partner's head, etc. Of course, this always corresponded with his hating to get his ears disinfected, often because of the tumour. He was sensitive and squeamish about any treatments on his face. After the nurses would leave his room, Jack would often scrub my Giraffe ears vigorously, with Dr. Cauli-flower egging him on. Some days, when he had homework to do, and wasn't feeling too motivated, he'd just yell at me (for being so stupid) and then he would work quite well. Or he would incite me to pour water over Dr. Chip's head from behind and then take Chip's side so that they both would scold La Giraffe! About twice a year my secretary tells me: "Your Uncle Jack called to say that he is doing quite well."

Sporting red noses, "Uncle" Jack and Alice, now re-baptised with a clown name, Dr. Ratatouille, join our morning parade. When they aren't pulling my tail and hiding it under a mattress, dunking it in a trash can or using it as a horse whip, they chase each other from corner to corner, shaking maracas, doing the hokey pokey and teasing nurses. Our mini platoon manages to perform two successful red-nose transplants on the new batch of medical students, who even relax enough to dance an improvised samba. Parents wander into the hallways, nurses stop for a few precious seconds. "The Halls are Alive with the Sound of Music....la la di daaaaaa......."

Coco-a-Gogo and I choose intellectual food to feed 14 year old Antoine, and for the "plat de resistance", it's Shakespeare! We interpret a romantic sonnet that begins: "Shall I compare thee to a summer's day? Blablablablabbla." Just wearing spectacles and moustaches, we keep the tone sober. For dessert we play a Bach duet on our flutes.

Antoine listens politely, yawns at least twice, while mom gets a moist twinkle in her eye. If we go down this route with him, maybe one day we will be able to drive on to the main road and get silly. He's (silently) screaming for more action but censors himself severely. And poetry and classical music suits us just fine.

In the B.M.T.U., we run into a doctor rushing out the door on his way to the airport, lugging a cooler in which he will retrieve a bone marrow donation in New York City later that night. Clutched in his hand is a drawing from an 8 year old, made especially for her B.M.T. "angel" in America. In bright pastels, a lithe blond girl sits under a tree full of red fruit. Facing her, a dog barks with a zillion hearts coming from his muzzle, floating into the sky, forming a glowing halo around his head. It's complex but straight to the point. I have rarely seen such poetic gratitude. In less than 36 hours, a simple anonymous gift of life will flow into the child's body. Back in the U.S.A., will people wonder, "where did that lovely drawing on the fridge come from?" And the donor will smile, saying, "This is from my 'secret' niece in France." But she (or he?) might think, "Did it work, is the kid alive?"

Louie has just received his transplant using his younger sister's marrow. Is this how we become bonded or indebted for life to a loved or resented sibling, or how we become "family" with a complete stranger? It reminds me of being pregnant when I had felt someone else's chemistry entering mine; I remember not being completely "me" anymore. It must also be confusing for my Lou. The empty bag hangs eerily on his wall, like a lion's head after the safari, a strange trophy. The tenacious struggle with "Lara Croft" is not over, now the real fight for survival and identity begins.

My thoughts drift to his healthy, little sister, now in a hospital bed with her backside feeling like a pincushion after the doctors extracted the marrow. She will be sore for a few days. Who will comfort her if the transplant doesn't take? If Lou dies, how will she cope? Is it a gift of life?

Given the circumstances, we try a peaceful clown-approach to no avail. His brown eyes are glued to a computer combat; grandma is knitting. Each to his own routine. Only a comic conflict can coax Lou's focus away from the laptop. All four of my limbs end up entangled in a chair while Coco-a-Gogo inflicts a myriad of small tortures on my hind parts. Behind the thick sheets of plastic, our fuzzy-headed lad looks up chortling and luxuriating in our kinetic predicaments.

45.

Excuses

"I am sorry. Je m'excuse." No one ever says these "Three Little Words" in a hospital. And if they do, I've rarely heard it. However, clowns say it all the time. Their mere entrance into a room reveals a personalised brand of blatant social imperfection, verbal ineptness and physical blundering. So what's better or funnier than to say: "I'm sorry", especially when nothing has fallen, broken or even happened yet. It's our calling card.

Doctors too, need to cope and survive. In a cancer ward, they must announce hundreds of difficult things year round and nothing except experience prepares them for these challenging tasks. Constantly saying they are sorry for an illness or even their failure to cure it, would probably be the rocky road to suicide or chronic depression. But when he feels the need (usually instinctively), the clown can take it on himself to "play" with the notion of apology; thus indirectly helping the medical staff.

My clown "husband" of the day is Dr. Bob, Yann. He's been working in the company now since early fall, but he is still "green" around the edges. His candid way of seeing the work is refreshing and puts an old trooper like La Giraffe onto her toes. He takes risks that no one with experience would ever dare and I adore that, but sometimes we pay the price of the puppy jumping, paws first into the bowl of milk. As usual, we start in high gear. Like myself, Dr. B. loves to play with anything and everything in sight to feed a comic situation. This makes for a two-headed red-nosed tornado that descends upon the ward with mischief!

In the B.M.T. U., there is a new boy "caged" behind the plastic curtains in room #4. The nurse describes his illness as an emergency. He has a rare condition that means that if he doesn't get an emergency treatment in the next week, he could die. She adds that his mama is "in a state of hysteria" but that, Kevin, a handsome boy, is coping rather well. Both are confined to a tiny space with a minimum of sterilised toys, a few books and a T.V. Through the door's window, Dr. Bob and I see a placid 7 year old sitting cross-legged on the bed playing with colourful Lego's. His mom looks like a salt statue, masked, booted and gowned, staring blankly into space. She might be slow to warm up to us but we are use to these types of situations, and know not to focus too much on her. Seems like a piece of cake! Maybe we can win her over by just making the boy smile.

The first thing that catches our eye upon entering that room is a ratty bear wedged behind a water pipe. The bear is on "our" side of the plastic curtain. He has not been subject to sterilisation procedures yet. He has no eyes, no mouth and no nose; just scars criss-crossing his whole body. This thing has already been through countless battles and the wounds have been stitched up dozens and dozens of times with a rainbow of coloured threads. There isn't much stuffing left on the inside either. The bear is here for an unprecedented battle and needs to join the boy soon.

From age nine months to five years, my daughter Lailah's favourite "doodoo" ("the nangy") was a chartreuse, satin edge of a blanket. Sometimes I would find it stuffed up her nose, wrapped tightly around her sucking thumb or just under the pillow. She kept losing it, which drove me insane and we shared many a giggle about just how "stinky" the nangy was. Kids decide when they must separate from these smelly morsels, not us. They adore it when the clown pays special attention to their doo doo and cherish all the variations on a theme that we invent for it to play. Sometimes the doo doo goes on a "journey", sometimes it just "acts up" and will "pee" on mom's head. If we use it as a puppet, sometimes it talks back. I often sense the gravity of this kind of play.

To Kevin's sheer delight, I start to "talk" to his bear and make a grotesque grimace because of his "odour". We get our first laugh. Dr. Bob picks up the pace and invites the bear to fly around the room as I pick "it" up and throw "it" into the air a few times. Second laugh. Bob catches the bear and starts to fly him up and down in the room, exploring all kinds of medical objects, instruments, I.V. poles and pumps. More giggles. This is a creative way to soften the harsh aspects of medical paraphernalia for a new arrival. Kevin is thrilled. He giggles, all bright-eyed and laughs with passion. Mom seems genuinely pleased to see her son full of enjoyment. Bob ups the stakes with the bear and accelerates the flying speed so that Mr. Bear is now crashing into objects, walls and even a certain Giraffe's bum. A mindful improviser, Dr. Bob notices a hook on the ceiling air vent and makes an impulsive decision to suspend the bear on the hook, as if Mr. Bear is in a permanent state of flight. Too late. The image of a lynched bear plunges a cold knife into our hearts as Kevin bursts into a frenzied sob. Mom dives onto the bed, arms protecting Kevin from the cruel world that seems to be making war on him. And now the bear, her son's dearest toy, looks murdered. And we are responsible.

Dr. Bob unhooks the bear. We freeze, suspended in our guilt, in awe of this tragedy that we have somehow ignited. I feel we have ambushed ourselves! Shot in the hoof. My inner voice of experience says to just let the child cry. We have triggered such grief in him that it is much bigger than all of us and that there is no time now for analysis or compensation. We must let a solution appear.

60 interminable seconds later, I say: "On your knees Dr. Bob. Now say you're sorry! Right away, oooost! And get a hop on it!" Bob obeys instantly, as a good clown must and Kevin slowly lifts his head, tears streaming down flushed cheeks. Thank god mom doesn't have resentment written all over her face. Bob: "I'm soooo sorry. Kevin, I'll never do that again. Never. Not even if you make me. I promise." Kevin's

breathing begins to slow down. Giraffe: "You are not sorry enough, Mr. Bob. Can you say that again, in 10 different languages and flat on your belly?" Kevin is calming down by the second and a gorgeous smile begins to materialise on his face. The clowning evolves into a full-fledged "punishment" of Bob, complete with fake clown slaps, phoney punches, taunting and revenge. I have experience! We leave a smiling mother and child, who both seem released.

I know that we had been right to have gone all the way with a thoughtless error. Sometimes, whether we like it or not, our clowning can push a child off an emotional shelf where he is holding on to stressful feelings of frustration, apprehension and rage. If he expresses his emotions during the play it can help soften the guilt he experiences; for making his parents feel sad and worried. Subsequently, I have one unhappy clown partner on my hands at lunchtime and I need to use the break to help Yann realise what a gift he has given Kevin, mom and ourselves.

It only hits us while in the dressing room that we have created a powerful metaphor for our patients. "SORRY". Sorry for the many hurts, the relapses, the unspoken fears, hospitalisations, impending chemos, radiation, nausea. Sorry for all the solitude. Our global "apology" had been heard and accepted by both mom and Kevin, and maybe they could face a round of boxing with illness.

The clown in his playing often becomes for the child, what D.W. Winnicott refers to as a "Transitional Object" (something like the doo doo that first helps a child separate from his mother). As a result, the clown-doctor plays an important part in enabling the child to separate his illness from himself. All too often children spend their time during an illness being defined by the illness. Unfortunately, as a consequence the child loses his sense of self as a healthy person. He is no longer John, who happens to have leukaemia, rather John sees himself only as a leukaemia patient. The clown-doctor helps to redress this inequity not only for the child with an illness but also for the hospital staff, and most importantly, for the child's parents.

At other times the clown performs an important role for children who are just too sick to engage in what Peter Slade calls "Personal Play", (for example when a child becomes a plane travelling noisily at great speed). At these times the clown-doctor is no longer just a transitional object; he is a toy to play with. Clown-doctors enable the sick child to engage in "Projective Play" where the clown becomes an object to be played with.

As one of the first rules of clown-doctoring is to "accept the gift", the child can control the clowns either directly, through language or gesture (as when a child uses Dr. Bob as a human jukebox), or indirectly with the compliance of one of the clowns (for example when a child gets La Mouche to pour water on Dr. Giraffe) So, although they

138

may be powerless to control their illness or the hospital procedures that are done to them, in their play the sick child is empowered because they have control over their clown toys. Moreover, in doing so the child is now part of the clown team.

46.

"La vie en rose"

Our weather lady says: "Fog, swirling winds turning into a storm warning."

It's going to be a stimulating day with Ami, Dr. Balthazar. We give ourselves a few goals: stay minimalists; make simple choices; keep distance on each situation; and, produce as little noise as possible. When clowns make too much fanfare, I smell anxiety. Our own. What can we be compensating for? We usually cause a fair amount of racket, ranging from poetic serenades and upbeat storytelling to boisterous clamour during hallway parades. We are rarely inaudible.

A doctor once compared putting up with clown noise levels to tolerating painful medical procedures: "You must balance between intensity and duration." It was a sobering lesson. We're always struggling to temper our sound levels to the climate and moods of the units. It's impossible, but the effort is worth cultivating. Complaints from staff are common in the beginning of a hospital program (marriage) and we are attentive not to overstep the limits of tolerance. We attempt to address each complaint individually and encourage dialogue. A muted, hushed and censored clown is no fun. The voice is one of our essential means of communicating joy. A happy child usually makes tons of sounds, even noise. However, when a performer is getting slightly burnt out and needs to be self-protective, he can create too much racket and needs to push the pause button! Then it is high time for self-evaluation and some external supervision from a clown spouse who has the courage to call a "Time Out".

The day starts off in front of the welcome wagon with Alice, Martin (just in for a blood test in the day clinic) and Giraffe playing catch with Balthazar's cap. First, it accidentally falls to the floor and becomes a personal crisis for Dr. B. . Mimi grabs the cap and throws it over to Alice while Balthazar drops flat on his face trying to intercept. Martin, still bundled up in a coat, waddles over to take the cap from Alice and makes a pass to Giraffe who sails it back to Alice. We keep Balthazar spinning and tumbling until Martin makes a run for it, tottering down the hallway with the cap and plunges smack onto his belly. He's gotten so plump that I almost think he will bounce back. He falls right in front of the doctors' aquarium. Everything stops. Tin-tin lets out a wail from the depths of his soul. A crowd gathers. Balthazar wants to laugh so hard, he has to hide. Dr. Dora quickly checks Martin out then gives him a long bear hug. It turns out that the little guy is more insulted than injured; that by running, he has also touched on what he is barely able to do physically. Balthazar's a sport and lets Tin-tin wear his cap for the whole morning.

Folded into a fetal position, head under the blankets and sucking her thumb, Ophelia has gone into hiding. There are two cranky grandmas on either side of the bed gossiping, as if the kid is absent. "Knock, knock." We hear "blablablabla" and wait, but there's no answer, the chit-chatting doesn't stop. So Balthazar slowly opens the door a crack and our two red noses peek in.

Grandma #1: "Go away, we don't have the heart to laugh right now."

Giraffe: "Uh....O.K. Granny but what about Ophelia?" (I see itty-bitty movements under the covers.)

Grandma #2: (grumble grumble)" Ophelia is too sick, can't you see, she is ILL!"

(We can see a small body shifting positions under the blanket.)

These are moments when good professionals have to take a deep breath and make a decision; either, be good clowns and respect the Grandmas' wishes (and go away), or be naughty clowns and enter the room; so that we do not abandon Ophelia in her solitude under the covers, enduring Granny gossip. We must risk taking a flying leap off the old theatrical cliff, praying that a parachute will open, the head nurse is not observing and that we will land on soft sand.

Giraffe: "WOOO! WOOOOOO! I'm not afraid of you GRAND-MAAA!"

(Ophelia is peeking at the scene now)

Balthazar: "Boo! Boo! Boo! You don't scare me either Mammy-poo!"

Grandma #1: "Well booooooooo to you too, clownie-wownies. I am the big bad wolf and I'm gonna eat you up for lunch!"

Grandma #2: howls like a wolf and starts chasing us with a salt shaker!

Grandma #1: picks up a fork and knife to join the chase!

(a hearty giggle crescendos from the bed).

Balthazar and I cannot believe our eyes. Just when we think we are risking a life sentence for offending two cantankerous old ladies, (in mourning) their sense of humour wakes up and they decide to have some fun. If you don't try you'll never know. Second miracle of the moment: Ophelia sits up in bed, ready for a glorious fight between her watch dog mammies and her mischievous clowns! We should have known that those two old biddies are all bark and no bite. Ophelia knows. Now can I hire the 2 of them?

What we do afterwards is of no great importance. Our two elderly assistants dance a mock ballet, then we juggle oranges over their gray heads, singing timeless songs: "La vie en rose", then "C'est Si Bon, si bon, si bon...". Ophelia, who knows all the words, sings along, allowing herself to have pleasure, even when she is "sick" and living through a bleak period. Perhaps this pleasure provides her with a message of hope and light at the end of the dark tunnel.

In the even better news department: Louie is leaving the B.M.T.U. and going home, which means that his transplant worked and that he had no complications. We also saw Rosa, who popped in for a quick check-up. Her hair has all grown back now past her ears and she is still her old self, full of piss and vinegar. The staff gathered around her making a fuss over her curls. She says to a nurse before leaving the day clinic: "The first time I saw the clowns, I thought they were tictoc!"

47.

Dr. Dora, Dr. Sam, Dr. Balthazar and Co.

This day is rich with many layers of adventures. I do not know where to start. There are at least five clown-miracles from sunrise to sunset. On such occasions, I need to find a way to digest all the events, let them speak wisdom to this blank page. For once I will try to capture the door to door journey:

9:00 A.M.: Ami and I have coffee with the head nurse and two doctors join us to discuss Ophelia's situation, then off to get the weather report from Mimi: "The sky is blue, there will be light." The head nurse immediately contradicts: "and there will also be moments of freezing rain..." What are we to think?

9:30 A.M.: The patient update comes from Dr. Sam. We note that there is a new 6 year old boy with a bad prognosis; a newly diagnosed 5 year old African girl (the mom has four other kids at home and will probably not be around much); plus, news on about 20 other patients. Scribble, scribble, I always take notes in code on a tiny pad to review during the day and to know what trouble we can get into. The codes are to respect medical secrecy on the rare chance that if the note pad ever got lost, no one would know of who or what I was talking about. For example: If a kid has an even temper I write: =; if he is moody I write: /\/\/; or if he is at life's end: (!). etc.

9:45 A.M.: We go back to the dressing room to read last week's journal notes, do vocal warm-ups, plot some theatrical strategy and set some priorities with patients. Then, into our make-up and costumes. I see that Balthazar has another new cap!

10:00 A.M.: We lead sober parades with ukulele and flute tunes: Irish, African, Hebrew, Italian, and a Caribbean one. No vocals, just our instruments.

10:15 A.M.: First stop to see a little pal who is obsessed with the Peter Pan story and who will only play with us impersonating, "Captain Hook." I try out my Wendy character and Balthazar plays the crocodile, who has just swallowed the alarm clock. Tic-toc-tic-toc-tic-toc. Mom is a mess, seems fed up with her child who says he is afraid of us. He seems to be enjoying himself. Perhaps we should have cast her as the crocodile. The kid spends 5 minutes, happily cutting us to pieces with his plastic dagger. Driiiiiing drrrrrring!

10:30 A.M.: Louie is in the day clinic and at Dr. Dora's request we stay to help him through a Lumbar Puncture: "I prescribe some clown anaesthesia for that kid..." Children claim that this medical exam is fairly painful despite the use of the M.E.O.P.A (a sort of anaesthesia). It certainly scares most of them. And me. We are getting more and more requests from the staff, parents and kids to be present during all kinds of procedures. Since we feel that we do not have the right to fail, the debate about whether clowns should or should not be included has been hot. Some clowns, like La Mouche can't stand the sight of a needle and blood or cope with a suffering child's cries. Then it's an easy call. She won't participate. Others, like myself have worked at finding our place during these challenging medical interludes.

Blowing bubbles for 15 minutes and playing calm, slow music are not the most interesting or creative performance activities for an advanced clown-doctor, but in the case of helping a child to cope with an invasive medical procedure, nothing is more useful. The child might understand that pain and fear are not a bottomless pit.

11:00 A.M.: Everything goes well with Louie; now the boy is almost a hospital pro. Dora asks if we can help out again with another boy's L.P. We say no. The problem with him is just the opposite to Louie. He laughs at us so hard, that he would move during the injection and that would be a catastrophe. The best thing we can do is to distract his mom, who gets upset during these procedures. So a big parade is in order with some other straggling moms, all of us singing Mozart's "Lucicare" and adding Caribbean percussion to keep things moving.

11:30 A.M.: It's time to give the bi-weekly "shower" to Alice's mom's feet. We call them, "the twins, Tovie and Nikki." We invent all kinds of adventures for the 2 feet and dress them up in doll clothes. Alice adores this ritual we have created for her and mom. Some kids want constant variety in play, others seem to need their stabilising rituals. This is similar to children who want to hear the same story over and over again. Comforting routines and order are important to all children; it provides structure for their lives. When hospitalisation disrupts this order, and in addition, gives children few choices, small rituals become critical.

Then on to meet two new patients: one, age six and the other, age four. We keep it simple and stupid - a few bubbles, some magic and a small party with Lili the mouse.

1:00 P.M.: Pizza is delivered to the nurse's lounge where we meet with Dora and Sam for lunch. We have become unusually attached to these two and have weathered good and bad times together. We think it is time to pass on some of our skills. Ami and I have prepared a surprise for them, three pocket props each and a clown lesson to teach them how they can work. First come the squeakers which you have to "palm" and then work on the co-ordination of the illusion. No one gets it right the first time, maybe like an injection. Then comes a mini magic wand and finger puppets, a cow for Dora and, a spaniel for Sam. (Where's my mouse?) We teach them how to work with the puppets, especially practising on where to focus their eyes. They are like 5 year olds playing and every time a nurse enters the lounge they try out their squeakers on various body parts.

1:45 P.M.: Before going back to the dressing room to freshen up our make-up and brush our teeth, the four of us devour an entire box of Belgium chocolates, a gift from a grateful family.

2:00 P.M.: We enter the B.M.T.U., put on our special garb, then scrub hands and sterilise a few props. We get a nurse's report on 5 patients to see.

2:15 P.M.: A teenage boy plays a video game with Balthazar who loses twice, but not on purpose. They make an appointment for next time so Balthazar can lose again. Three red-nosed rules for clown-doctors: #1. always say YES to a proposal from a child or a partner; #2. A clown's "flop" is usually funnier to the audience than a success; and, #3. Make sure your standards are high so you can bomb in style.

2:30 P.M.: We play a ballad for a medical secretary who looks depressed. We must have triggered a painful memory because she loses it and cries. We really didn't mean to provoke this and feel embarrassed until she starts to giggle through her tears. Maybe the music helped her liberate a well-buried wound. Then take a break to exchange bawdy jokes and a few songs with the B.M.T.U. nurses in their lounge. They've had three adult patient deaths in their unit this week and need the diversion plus some gallows humour. We're better at the bawdy material.

3:00 P.M.: One of the nurses requests that we pay a clown call on an English speaking, adult in the B.M.T.U., who was about to be taken to the I.C.U.; that he was quite anxious. The nurses dared us to visit this guy, saying that he had horrendous behaviour with everyone. "Tell him he has just won La Giraffe in a lottery!" I love a challenge and any opportunity to be a "star" so I let Balthazar take a back seat to play my lighting technician! The man was as sweet as peaches and cream with me after a few seconds of pure flirtation and a personalised version of "I wanna be loved by you, just you and nobody else but you..."! Maybe he just needed to be sung to in his native tongue and a few spoons of coquette-syrup before being wheeled away. It did seem to reassure him. We cannot usually spare the time to visit adults, but once in a while we welcome getting kidnapped.

3:15 P.M.: We take off our sterile costumes and stick them into the washing bin. Then run into half a dozen members of Alice's family in the hallway and get them to waltz to "The Blue Danube", with tons of musical side effects à la Spike Jones.

3:30 P.M.: Balthazar and I pull off a full-fledged Marx Brothers' routine for a small boy with a bloated tummy and a hearty belly laugh. We slam in and out of the closets and bathroom with a new partner, one of the nurses. She plays the "scolding" white clown, to our two augustes. Because I end up with 20 coat hangers stuck on different limbs, she has lots of chiding to do. She eventually puts them all back into the closet as she bursts into laughter and runs to change an I.V. bag of medication.

4:00 P.M.: We perform wild belly dancing with a pre-teen girl and her family of Moroccan women. Balthazar sings and gets goofy on his ukulele, playing zanier notes and chords (sounds like the Arabian blues). An older lady, with a traditional scarf on her head and a gold-toothed smile insists on slipping us a folded 20 franc bill. It's a customary Mid-eastern way of thanking performers and putting a stop to the chaos. Despite our code of ethics, we cannot refuse, it would be an insult in their culture. The whole time, I can't get Jasmin out of my mind.

4:45 P.M.: A toddler won't stop crying unless "her" clowns come to "her" room so one of the nurses panics, looking all over for us. We had been lost on an expedition to Mars in another room. So the last 15 minutes of the day is spent with the tyke, her nurse and auntie, singing all their favourite songs. As we walk to the locker room, a familiar melody perfumes the airs; "Au clair de la lune, j'ai peté dans l'eau, ca fasait des bulles, c'etait rigolo...."

5:15-6:00 P.M.: Our throats are so dry that Ami and I both need to drink a quart of water; we change into our civvies; then, go to the nurse's lounge to write up the day's events in the clown journal. As we write and talk, Ami remembers a funny story and tells it to me: "Dr. Zel and I had a nice morning in the oncology ward, and we sat down to eat lunch with some nurses in their lounge. Suddenly, the door opens and a nurse runs in panting: "The Professor is looking for the clowns, it's quite urgent."

Zel: "What's up?"

Nurse: "He's about to do an Lumbar Puncture on a little girl."

Balthazar: "So...?"

Nurse: "Well, the kid doesn't want to hear anything about it unless the Professor wears a red nose while giving her the needle...." Everybody in the lunchroom is smiling..." Ami continues," So I (Balthazar) take a clean red sponge nose and place it in a yellow plastic bag, then inside a red plastic bag, and then inside a green plastic bag and when I'm satisfied that the nose is suitably prepared, I give it to the nurse. She rushes off with the precious "organ" that is about to be transplanted onto her boss's face."

"So what about the nose? Did the Professor wear it?", I ask. We never really found out but what really mattered was that the 'king' was willing to play the "fool" and that's one of the highest compliments that anyone has ever paid us!"

48

Crying Wolf with a Duck Call

I get to work with Dr. April today. He is La Giraffe's soul brother; both so naive and dumb, that it can be overwhelming for others. To try to balance this double-dose of stupidity, we have to establish our goals at the start of the day so that our manner becomes a luscious dance of fools rather than a bumbling jig of nincompoops. Today, one of our main goals is to create as little noise as possible and to let April do the steering. Being a brilliant, natural follower, leading is something he does not practice often. This gives me comic relief from responsibility in the ward, where I know everyone and am supposedly the stupidvisor.

After those long weeks in the B.M.T.U., followed by a period at home to eat pizzas and teach his little sister the art of killing computer outlaws, our Louie is back again with a small infection that has everyone worried.

In the playroom, he has found a plastic scooter made for 2 year olds and is creating a race in the hallways reminiscent of "Le Mans." Short of tying him down, there is no way anyone can convince him to stay in his room. A passing nurse sighs, then remarks: "You wouldn't know that this one belongs here, he acts so normal." Louie seems so irrational, worried about something, and he is driving everyone nuts.

Each time Lou catches sight of me and Dr. April, we are entitled to a spray of "machine gun-fire" or just a simple grenade in the face. Mr. Wild Cat is on the loose. We fight back with flute fire and bubble bombs, stumbling over laundry bags, hiding under the front desk or diving for cover in the linen closets. Our small kid - clown war, treats the mere visitor walking into the ward to a scene of back alley brats bumping into walls, yelping insults: "Rotten Potato!; Farting lizards!; Elephant poo balls!" etc. And too bad for the odd one who thinks he is entering a silent leukaemia church, where pale children are on their death beds, learning to become angels. Not in our ward!

Around noon, Dr. April and I put on our tacky "sterilised" gowns, caps, and prepare to visit the 3 kids stuck in the B.M.T.U. When we come out an hour later, as usual, we go into the central bathroom to change back into our white coats and clown costumes. Alexis is feeling as hypoglycaemic as I am and we are both ready to faint or bite each other if we don't eat soon. As I try to push the door open, I hear a high pitched giggle. Some mysterious person is holding it shut! Has to be Lou.

"I've locked the clowns in the bathroom, (hee, hee, hee). Hey everybody, I've locked the clowns in the bathroom!", he screams with glee. Muffled nurse laughter filters through the door. Then follows no less than 15 minutes of negotiations and attempted bribery with one stubborn little boy who has captured two prisoners. He is not about to liberate us. Something is at stake, but we can not identify it. The door cannot be opened without hurting the little monster, so we have to be patient, try to figure out a new tactic for escaping and put up with the gnawing in our bellies. Somewhere in the back of our minds, we have confidence that someone will have some pity on us - hopefully today.

Dr. April manages to wedge his big foot into an opening in the door and creates a five inch gap. Lou doubles his war hoots and I blow on my duck call for help, knowing that I also risk getting into trouble with the nurses for "crying wolf" (with a duck call?) or making too much noise. At last Dr. Dora shows up and as simple as pie, Lou releases his prisoners. So we run to our salads and cheese while Louie and Dora have a private chuckle.

Who knows how long Louie could have lasted. His persistence is remarkable. Such patience. Idio-pathetic that I am, it only hits me in the dressing room that Lou has just celebrated his own release from the B.M.T.U.! He is free and what a jubilant feeling to lock the clowns up. It is his glorious revenge on the medical system. They have the audacity to lock little boys up just to save their lives! And who could have been a better liberator of the clowns, than Dr. Dora?

49

Two Beauti-fool Flowers Open

The affable Basket (Pierrette) and La Giraffe, are paired for the day. We work as complementary augustes on the loose. During our morning warm up, Pierrette and I decide to work on a comic musical number that involves choreographed precision and timing. Without synchronised movements we risk bloody noses and bruised egos. Our goal is to adapt each variation on the main musical theme, so as to play for babies, middle sized kids, professors, mamas, cleaning ladies, papas and teens. The instruments for our number are a flute, a slide whistle, a duck call and a kazoo.

The strongest moment of the day is with a lovely 3 year old girl, named Linda. A few soft, feathered strands of copper hair are still left on top of her crown. She is a fine-boned sparrow of a girl. She peoples her miniature games with princesses and kings, dragons and mermaids. Her pregnant mother is never far away. She learned of her pregnancy the week after her daughter was diagnosed with cancer. Dark-eyed, raven-haired Mama is imprisoned in a sadness that keeps her body tense and spirit unreachable. While reading our clown journal Pierrette tells me that the mom expressed right from the beginning of her child's diagnosis, a strong belief that her child will die. This is so rare. Even if parents fear death, they never say that they are certain of it happening.

Tiny Linda compensates for her mom's dark moods with a total commitment to fantasy and imaginative play. Our goal is to include the mom without creating additional tension or resistance. We do not want to get on her nerves and anyone can see she has a short fuse. This is high wire walking for clowns. It means that not only do we have to take great care not to overwhelm the child, but we cannot enter into direct contact with the mother. Mom turns her head away the whole time we use tiny finger puppets to entice Linda onto an island of imaginative play. The rubber dog puppets are perfect. They bark, growl, and pee on inappropriate objects (even into mom's fashionable purse). Slowly, our two flowers blossom. Mom simply observes her daughter playing and the child keeps a close check on her mamma's eyes to make sure she is not "mad." Like a tango, their 4 eyes keep making more and more contact as the games evolve. We leave them playing together, hardly noticing that the two clowns have left to walk their "dogs."

Afterwards, Basket and I have to take a ten-minute breather to crash, land and process the melancholy lake which we have just crossed. Ducking into an empty patient's room, we drink huge amounts of water in paper cups. We sigh, heave and give each other cross-eyed looks. We are beyond words. This usually gregarious duo is speechless. We

150

spontaneously hug each other. Emerging from our stupor, Pierrette and I agree that in both of our "clown doctor careers", we have rarely seen a heavier tragedy. It's not that other parents don't suffer horrendously, it's just that this woman would not let anyone reach her. Even her daughter. Today she let herself be touched and we saw a sliver of light appear behind her dark curtain of terror.

50

Back Home with the Clown-Doctors

Today is our monthly clown meeting. There are at least 24 out of 31 performers present. We will devote the entire day to exchanging ideas and stories about our work. Loving the work in the hospitals is not enough. It is essential to enrich our path with new ideas and provoke change. Obsessed with finding new techniques for helping the kids and for improving our clowning, I want to develop interactive ways of working with medical staff. Performers need more medical and creative training to adapt their art to hospital performing: classes on pain assessment, child development, bereavement and even anorexia.

Next month a doctor will teach us about pain, it's treatments and how to recognise symptoms in a hospitalised child. The month after we will have a master class in puppetry. These monthly encounters keep everyone in communication with each other and help us to keep our clown-doctoring techniques on the cutting edge. We have our own style of keeping our meetings running smoothly without too much chaos and people speaking all at once. There is always a designated fool.

Alex., (Dr. Zen) the newest addition to the company, is present. He's a 7th generation circus performer; an acrobat as well as musician, he has clowned since the age of five. He will be a kick in the seat of the pants for one and all. I chose him not just for his talent, but for his youth. He will bring balance to a group of experienced and sometimes over-serious performers. It is an intense experience to participate in our meetings. The majority of the clowns present have been working for L.R.M. at least seven years.

I deliver the news that we have gotten our grant back to work at a hospital where over 50% of the funding had been lost! It is a major victory for everyone, but especially for the hospital staff. Faced with losing the clown-doctor program, they circulated two petitions, one coming from their unit and another coming from the parents of hospitalised children! They collected hundreds of signatures calling for clowns!

After brainstorming ideas for performing in the evening at the hospitals (wearing nightgowns, singing lullabies, etc.) the clowns start to discuss their most recent joys and losses. There have been several deaths in our hospitals this week so the conversation is weighted.

Somehow we drift onto the subject of medical secrecy and the different attitudes in each hospital. One of the great dilemmas for an artist working in a hospital is the question of confidentiality. Since we are neither therapists nor do we take the Hippocratic oath, something had to be done to ensure respect for medical secrecy, and thus win the trust of a hospital team in order to work with quality, on a long term basis with "their" patients.

Is it necessary for a clown to know if a child is in pain, has been molested, about to have a limb amputated or has an incurable disease? Yes. Experience tells us that to remain 100% sensitive, avoid making mistakes and to perform appropriately for each medical case, it is critical for a performer to modify his gestures or actual physical distance from a patient or even question the choice of a song. A child deserves no less.

In a paediatric ward with seriously ill children, it is imperative that the usual anarchy and imaginative process of the artist - clown be respected while requiring him to obey a few basic principles. There are eleven basic "articles" in Le Rire Medecin's code of ethics. They set and define standards of professionalism, boundaries of artistic expression, limits of the creative role, responsibility of each artistic act, respect for patients as well as healthcare workers, privacy, emotional parameters and distance on patients, political positioning, basic safety and even hygiene. Most clowns who have worked for Le Rire Medecin feel that the code provides them with a solid frame and thus frees them to create. It enables us to maintain a policy of professional discipline, honest craftsmanship and creative generosity.

We ask simple things; for example: "Is the child in pain?; Is she or he blind or deaf?; Do the parents visit?; etc. A doctor once refused to tell us anything about the kids because she was afraid we wouldn't be capable of seeing what was well in the child afterwards. We managed to reason with her. Another time, we had to leave a ward and stop a program because the nurses refused to understand the importance of a decent report. A million meetings got us nowhere. In another unit the nurses just give us the bare minimum - "he has a blood problem, no visits from family and he's depressed." From that, we might assume that the child is HIV positive and that he has lost a parent. It is better to know more, so as to avoid any blatant mistakes, and to let the child know that we are all part of a team rooting for his health!

I remember a conversation with two nurses who have worked with us for over eight years in the cancer ward. Like the doctor who had refused information, they were concerned about whether we could really be "in the mood" to perform and stay spontaneous after hearing grim news at a staff meeting. I had to insist that we were trained, professional performers who knew how to work with the information we were receiving. Good theatrical training enables us to distance ourselves from the emotions of our character's situation. We are skilled at drawing a line between fiction and reality and can use reality to enhance fiction. I gave examples on preparing a "character" from my brief New York film and stage career. After explaining all this, one of the nurses pipes in: "Oh so you're a real actress, a method actress?" It is important that staff have confidence in us as well as understand our goals and techniques.

The subject drifts back to medical secrecy. We discuss a good example of why knowing the case history of a patient can be important; how we once teamed up with a psychologist in an adolescent unit, where we have always gotten excellent nurse's reports. We heard about a 12 year old boy who had just been hospitalised for behaviour problems, a year after he had been sexually abused by an uncle. The uncle was in jail and the trial was coming up. My partner Stephie (Dr. Josephine) and I decided to treat the boy as though he was a guest in a hotel; after all he was not physically sick!

When we arrived at his room, he was tucked under the covers like a good patient, watching T.V. Our clowning centred around skilfully turning the T.V. off, so that he could focus on our arrival and welcoming him to our "auberge", asking a number of questions about his preferences from today's "Clown Menu".

Dr. Josephine: "On today's menu, we offer: a salad of rap music; a soup of jokes; a main course of juggling frogs; and, a dessert of tall tales. Would you like to pick something in particular?"

Boy: "Jokes."

Giraffe: "Right, hear about the bla bla bla ....?" After hearing my joke, the boy smirked and said: "I have a better joke."

Dr. Josephine: "Go for it. "

He proceeded to tell two jokes: First a racist one about Africans; it is far from being politically correct, especially for a kid of Arab descent. We tried to stay fairly neutral and non-judgemental. And then he told a vulgar joke about "a youngster who gets solicited by a paedophile. And as he runs away to "safety" he gets tricked by a truck driver, who then rapes him." After hearing this, Dr. Josephine and I could not move or utter a sound for a full minute. The kid clearly wanted to know our reaction to his second joke. All I could say was, "shit happens kid. It wasn't funny, was it?"

Later in the afternoon, we went to the psychiatrist's office to relate our troubling experience with the boy and to see if we could exchange points of view. We wanted to know if we are hurting or helping the situation. According to the doctor, "this kid had never been able to express his feelings about the abuse and always refused to talk about the straight facts. He offers you two twisted jokes, because he knew that you would not judge him, shame or betray him. With the first joke, the boy tricked you into listening to him and was careful to test your reactions. With the second joke, he delivered his message (about his own trauma)." The psychiatrist was relieved that the boy was beginning to find his way towards communicating, even if it was with...clowns.

Our monthly meeting continues until early evening with a dozen more stories, a few tears and much shared laughter. There is a great bistro around the corner so we finish the day with a good glass of Bordeaux.

51.

National Poetry Week

Mimi says that the sky is clear, but that anything can happen. It is National Poetry Week and the entire French nation celebrates the springtime with the language of Baudelaire: in schools, cafes, theatres etc. Ready for all poetic emergencies, Nadine and I leave the locker room with a few books in our pockets: Beckett, Verlaine, Groucho Marx and Shakespeare's Romeo and Juliet. As soon as we hit the hallways, we take phrase samplings from everyone we can lay a hand on. They contribute sometimes with enthusiasm, and sometimes with long thoughts before speaking. By noon, almost 30 people have participated; nurses, doctors, parents and kids of all ages. We write each phrase onto colourful post-its and stick them up on the walls and doors so the place begins to look crazy. Good thing the Queen Bee is on vacation.

A 3 year old shows up with a one centimetre of downy hair, making her seem like an oversized infant. Her mom took us aside and told us, "My daughter said she wanted her 'baby' dolls to look just like her so before coming to the hospital she trimmed all the hair off their heads." So I wondered silently, when her hair grows back, will the dolls sprout new hair?

Ophelia is back for a new round of chemotherapy. She is still clearly in mourning for her mom and suffering from that "too good, too polite" syndrome; alone and passive. We read poetry, she listens and that is good enough.

We haven't seen Louie for a week, but the journal had notes saying that he was hospitalised again with high fevers. Today Lou looks thinner, a grey colour invading his skin and his eyes are slightly sunken, too dull. I do not like that skin colour. "Play it again, Sam." All his play is based upon war. As long as he needs the metaphor and the physical, emotional outlet, it's going to be just that, war. I'll never get tired of getting killed by Lou. I admit that I have no idea how to break this pugilistic pattern but the little guy is really not doing well. So we will indulge him.

No Rimbaud in this room, it's more like Rambo! He squirts us with water from a syringe and pretends to shoot us with a machine gun. He persists with great energy and mom supplies him with bowls of water to fill the syringes. This reminds me of when I was four and would gather bags of acorns for my brother's garbage pail wars in the neighbourhood against the "bad" boys. I felt like Florence Nightingale. Maybe Lou's mom needed to feel useful too.

Before going to other rooms, we decide to play "re-decorators", rearranging the furniture, turning the place upside down. La Mouche

156

seems proud of her Home-Beautifool touch. Despite his love of chaos, Lou is not completely pleased. As revenge, he steals my flute while I am not looking, so I am forced to steal his snacks. We trade back because he is hungry and I need the flute. Maybe we should put his stuff back? A new game: "re-establishing order."

At the end of the day Nadine and I leave the ward chanting Diane's poem: "Love...sung. Love...danced. Love...pierced. Love...gone."

Fools have always disturbed order. Medieval fools mocked Kings and Bishops because in part it was fool's "job" to disrupt everyday routines and rituals. The fool did not always understand why he did what he did, he disrupted things because he could and because it made people laugh. However in doing so he always ran the risk of going too far and either losing the king's favour or his own head.

In a similar way most modern clown-doctors know that disturbing a child's orderly routines will almost always upset someone. However they also know that sometimes disrupting a routine is necessary in order to break a pattern of "destructive" play or a cycle of inappropriate behaviour or simply to try to stimulate a new way of communicating with the child.

To achieve these goals clown-doctors will often physically rearrange furniture and personal belongings or deliberately disorganise a room as part of their play. This disruption to the status quo may create new growth in the clowns' interactions with the child. However, before they leave the room they must consider the child's emotional state. Some kids can cope with the chaos, others can't. When the clown-doctor creates mayhem he must consider the negative as well as the positive effects it might have on the child. Sometimes he has to do some housework before leaving or help clean up the mess after the disruption to routine. The beginnings of another game?

52.

Reverse Psychology

Mimi says: "I am personally in outer space, but the clouds will soon evaporate and let the sun shine brightly." Mimi is hardly ever wrong! The joint is jumping with kids."

Soon afterwards, La Mouche and I are running in circles with Alice and good old "Uncle Jack" on our tails. Why is he back so soon? Imagine the sound of children giggling and skittering with each other. It happens to be a rare sound in a leukaemia ward, but less so lately. We imitate King Kong and Godzilla monsters and run up to Louie's mom trying to scare her. Her response: "Because of everything I have been through, I am not scared of anything, or anybody and certainly not clowns!"

Dr. Sam asks us to entice a wee one into the hallways now that she can officially leave isolation. She has a serious case of "stare at the ceiling, pick the nose - syndrome", which is logical after 7 weeks of being shut up. The mere idea of walking into the big bad hallway, is frightening and does not feel safe. Also, those little legs are weak and her neurological system has been affected by the chemotherapy, so walking again does not feel secure.

Everyone was on the wrong side of the fence, trying in vain to seduce this irascible child to taste the pleasures of freedom. It is clear that the door on her "cage" has opened too abruptly for the child. A bit of reverse psychology was what Dr. Giraffe ordered. I just crouch at her side and whispered, that "we would not leave the room, we are tired and we are happy staying in the horizontal position. Everyone should leave us alone now." The girl is relieved that someone was at last of her opinion.

Later, when she sees that Uncle Jack and Alice are still racing around like lunatics, she gets up with the help of her mom and the Physiotherapist and shuffles towards the door to watch all the hallway action. Perhaps reverse psychology works.

The nurses tell us that Louie pretended to be sleeping this morning when they came in. Last night it took until 11 P.M. to "persuade" him to swallow his pills, so he had plenty of reasons to be groggy now. He's a stubborn mule too and still is looking pale and thin. Apparently there is a virus in his system that is not giving up. Keep fighting, sport.

We enter Louie's room as three nurses are trying to give him medication with a glass of orange juice. At one point we tie up his legs with paper streamers as if we have captured the HULK, in person. Of course, Louie displays his superior muscle power, breaks the "iron" chains and swallows his juice with the dreaded medication. We're all impressed. Later on La Mouche walks around the ward with a giant X taped onto her mouth. Lou's doings. "Mamie-Fart" got the same treatment. Are there things not being said?

NOISE! Besides the yearly debates on medical secrecy, this is what nurses and doctors love to complain about whenever we evaluate clown work in a hospital. At the meeting we conduct at the end of the day, the Professor says that he can still remember the days before 1983, when he was an intern. There were high levels of noise, crying and screaming in all paediatric wards. This was because all the blood tests etc. were done by injecting a needle directly into every kid's arm without any notion of treating pain. Nowadays, the children have I.V. lines, catheters or broviacs which permit them to have tests done without pain and without the skin being pierced each time.

In the mid 90's the healthcare teams started to use a cream that anaesthetised the skin before an injection and soon after that they started using a kind of laughing gas-anaesthesia for L.P.'s, myelograms and other invasive procedures. The Professor said that in the past, from 10 A.M. to noon everyday, there used to be the excruciating noise of wailing kids and that now, "maybe things have gotten too quiet." I think that he is brilliant. On that note, I read them the sound samples taken early last fall.

We all agree that in the near future, we should collaborate on a study. The most popular subject seems to be: "The advantages of clowns accompanying invasive medical procedures with children ages three - ten." Lately the nurses stay in the room with us after a difficult medical procedure on a kid, joining in a song or nutty routine. One girl actually applauded and thanked everyone after the P.L. needle came out; no one could believe their ears. We make a date to determine all the variables for protocol and collaboration. We even talk about making our own video or presenting our work at a conference.

After the meeting, La Mouche and I are asked to accompany two more medical procedures: first, an L.P. with the new 5 year old "wild-child" (or so the nurses say) and all goes surprisingly well thanks to Lili the mouse's musical antics (at one point she says with her sweet African accent: "Clowns, if you sing too loud the needle might break"); then during a blood test with Antoine, we serenade him with a Mozart duet while he conducts us with a coloured pencil and his mom relaxes in a chair. It seems to help the nurses cool out, especially after "l'enfant terrible".

A bit later we stick our noses through the door to see Miss wild child and she is in a foul mood. Her auntie has just finished braiding her hair into a multitude of pigtails and she looks like a queen. When we attempt to engage her in some play, she rejects us big-time! She demands stickers or "nothing." Because she refuses all interaction, we focus on her aunt (who responds with a tremendous laugh) while she yells: "You are not even playing with me, so go away!" When we try once more, she kicks us out again. It's a case of "damned if you do, damned if you don't." A classic in accepting rejection.

Martin is back (just for a quick L.P.) in the day clinic armed with a bright green wig and a "farting" prop which is terrific for grossing out the nurses. His clowning skills are evolving. The three of us create bed-pan-demonium. Upon hearing our clatter, another boy pops out of his room decked out as Zorro. With his plastic sword he "signs" bottoms with a "Z"! He and Tin-tin exchange props and the two rascals team up for the day.

Diane is in the B.M.T.U. and depressed about being cooped up for the next two months. While La Mouche "dances", I play a classical piece for her and we sing a few corny ballads. "Summertime and the livin' is easy...Fish are jumpin' and the platelets are low...." So nice to just let the kid relax and listen sometimes without any participation or chatting.

Before leaving for the day we pop in to check on Louie see that yes, he is back to his old fighting self, and now a rosier shade of grey. Granny Fart has just given him a new computer game with a "real" gun to shoot the bad guys. He gleefully massacres at least 300 gangsters on screen as we hover over him. When I ask where he puts the bodies, he points to the garbage can. The red curtain opens for our exit as the big Lou deploys a fierce spray of gunfire onto our bums, already stigmatised by Zorro. I notice a tray of brain teasers at the door, for everyone to try before setting foot into his room. His personal invitation to play. I've seen Lou do a few puzzles in a row with his eyes closed. I also see nurses secretly trying in vain to figure them out in the hallways. Even Dora can't do them and she's a smart doctor.

After getting out of costume and makeup, as I am sitting at the welcome wagon desk, talking on the phone with my office, Mr. Louie comes out of his room claiming triumphally: "Ah-ha, Ah-haaaaaa, now I see who you really are!" Unmasked.

53.

The Art of Observation

From time to time, I love to spend a day, inclownito, just watching others: the nurses, doctors, clowns, the parents, even the kids, working hard at being sick. There is an art to observation.

I have been invited by the Professor to share time with the staff in the B.M.T.U. . It seems essential to understand their daily rhythms of work and to acknowledge their expertise as healthcare professionals. My intention is to enrich the red nose - white coat knowledge pool and deepen the understanding of each other, in hopes of a more creative collaboration.

I was without clown makeup and costume, "disguised as a human", another variation on feeling naked. I admit to feeling awkward and intimidated by the hospital atmosphere without my red nose. This has not changed much in 14 years. I am dressed in monochrome beige, so as to politely disappear, to intermingle with dignity. It is a completely different feeling walking in the hallways without the slightest intention of entertaining. I feel unarmed and vulnerable. To my surprise, few people notice or recognise me, and that's just fine.

After eating lunch with the gang of nurses I run off to the B.M.T.U. . The staff meeting starts 15 minutes late, which is not a planetary surprise. At precisely 2:44 P.M., nine nurses (all female), the professor and the psychiatrist (sole representatives of the male kingdom) congregate in the small nurses station. The mood is calm, yet four soft-voiced conversations can be heard simultaneously. There are 10 cases to be discussed. Everyone seems comfortable with my presence. During these 75 minutes: The door opens and closes 47 times with someone going in or out; the telephone rings 11 times, followed by a conversation; the computer makes all kinds of strange noise; at least 22 "parallel" discussions take place in whispers; and, beepers go off 5 times.

Despite all these disturbances, and to my amazement the nurses, guided by the Professor get their work done in a calm, professional way. I cannot begin to imagine the insanity of a door opening and shutting 47 times during a clown meeting! Each child's emotional and social well-being is thoroughly discussed from a medical point of view. I am asked for my opinion in several instances. After I thanked the Professor for permitting me to participate, he asks if he could sit in on a clown-journal "pow-wow" in the nurses lounge at the end of the day. I am touched to the quick.

I leave the hospital singing to myself. It's a glorious day, summer has come to Paris and I would give anything for the children cooped up in the wards to feel the caress of sunshine on their pale skin.

Alora

54.

Emotions

I feel like a kid going to the circus, or getting ice cream on a hot day and am completely overexcited. Anne (Madame Cauli-flower) called last night, cancelling at the last minute and needing a substitute. Thinking I was going to spend the day at the office, I quickly digest the change of plan and am thrilled to jump into la Giraffe's skin, ready to visit the oncology ward. Plus, I get to work again with Basket, who has what I call, basic "joie de vivre." I am in total admiration of Basket for she really knows how to physically touch a kid. She takes some risks that no one in my company dares; tickling and poking, with a non-medical, non-parental, non-threatening touch! Her particular brand of rough-housing must be a relief for the kids, both from all the kisses and hugs they gets from worried parents and, from all the medical procedures inflicted on their bodies.

The nurses have warned us that there is a mom here who wants the clowns (and many other things) for her own needs. Her son has cancer and she is so panicked that all she can do is seek acknowledgement. She literally monopolises our attention and systematically answers all of the questions we ask her son. We finally manage to manipulate her into a chair (she starts to pout) and play for the boy. During a rock and roll moment created just for him (he's 11 years old going on 85), we want to "audition" a "go-go dancer." This is our clown-way of giving Mom a royal chance to participate. Basket and I try to recruit her, but she keeps sulking and refuses to move from the chair. Her son, exasperated, looks over his horn-rimmed glasses and states: "I have the unhappy honour to inform you that, this is my only mother and I haven't raised her correctly, so I'm sorry." Good thing he keeps his sense of humour.

There were days in our beginnings in France when the nurses would tell us not go into certain rooms. Dr. Cauli-flower and I always tried to comply but unceasingly asked why. The reasons could vary from emotionally raw parents, an approaching death, to an unsightly tumour. These were situations that the staff felt we couldn't handle. One time, the reasons were convincing: "The mother is suicidal, the teenage boy is in a coma and you jokers don't even know him." We took them at their word and proceeded to make our clown rounds.

In the midst of one of Madame Cauli-flower's grandiose magic numbers in a room with three patients and many visitors, a furious woman (the suicidal mom...) appeared at the door. All eyes turned to this human tornado and we held our breath. Were we making too much noise? Were we doing something offensive while her child was "dying"? "So," she blurted out, "Because my son, Henry is unconscious, does that mean that neither he nor I have the right to a clown visit?" The laughter was cut

164

short and all I could manage was a timid: "we'll be right there, m'am after we finish this magic trick. I prrrromise." I knew Cauli-flower was wondering if we were going to "get in trouble" with the nurses for "trespassing." We jumped off the comic diving board and decided to face the music if we had to. After all, the woman demanded our presence.

From our bumbling beginnings, for which we were quickly forgiven, the relationship with this mother and her boy evolved into a four month "love-affair." In the next months, we visited Michelle and her son twice a week. We never missed a Rendez-Vous. We saw them faithfully, sometimes singing old French songs for the mom, rap music for her son or joking about anything and everything under the hospital sun. Henry never woke up but Michelle, Cauli-flower and I believed that he always listened.

One day Cauli-flower and I decided to visit Michelle and Henry and to only play music. With my partner playing soft repetitive chords, I improvised a flute solo according to the room's vibe and then for some unearthly reason, started to play a few Hebrew melodies "from my youth." Michelle seemed pleased and Henry's breaths were regular and calm.

Days later as I emerged from the elevator, I saw a glassy-eyed Michelle. I expected the worse. She had been waiting for me. "Dr. Giraffe, you have to tell me what those melodies were that you played on Tuesday. I need to know. They have been haunting my nights. I cannot sleep." With obvious relief (that Henry was still alive), I explained that they were Hebraic tunes, that I had learned in synagogue as a kid and I hoped it hadn't offended her. I noticed that Michelle wore a gold cross on a chain around her neck and deduced that she was a devout Catholic. Then she replied: "Oh my god, that's what I thought. I reacted so emotionally to those tunes and I didn't understand why. I can still hear them in my dreams. You see, I know nothing about my past, really nothing, but I learned recently that I was of Polish-Jewish origins. My father admitted it to me on his deathbed. He had survived three years in a concentration camp and upon his release he vowed that his children would be baptised as Catholics so that they never would have to suffer as he had. Thank you and now go put on your nose."
*

At the end of the day and after miles of hallways, Basket and I have a heart-to-heart talk with Dr. Sam who is working in Oncology now. I am touched by how he describes the pain specialist, as a magical healer; a white witch! He admires anyone who can find the keys for alleviating children's pain. They are often self-critical perfectionists and rarely disparaging of a colleague, but never complimentary.

Most of the talk with Sam centres on a 6 year old boy, who is about to have a major operation on his face. His behaviour has been very difficult for the nurses to handle and he has been growling like a wild beast, threatening everyone that he is a wolf! His mom wants to take him back to her village one time before the disfiguring operation. She wants the family to see a "cute" kid, not a mutilated one. Sam tells us that the psychiatrist had a talk with the nurses and doctors to say that the boy was probably afraid of becoming a "monster", and that he was picking up clear messages from his mom and probably a few other people. This helped everyone deal with his behaviour and their own understandable reactions.

Sam couldn't speak of the medical procedure because he was too emotional. I have never seen him express real attachment to a child before. So to explain the operation to us, he did an unexpected pantomime. Are our methods rubbing off on him? Ten minutes without a word, his face suddenly alive with emotion, Sam shows us exactly how the surgeon will chop up the little jaw and replace it with pieces of a shin bone. We are floored. We have never experienced a non-verbal patient report before. We are touched. Could this be a real doctor talking? It turns my world upside down.

Seeing that Sam needs to focus on something lighter, we take him out of the nurse's station and involve him in some hallway parading. The little boy in question happens to be coming out of his room and also needs distraction. Basket shows him and the doctor a game on how to blow air into a clown, just like you would blow up a balloon. Guess who plays the balloon? When it gets nice and taut, you let all the air out and can laugh when the "balloon" pops and splatters onto the walls. The boy, his mom, a few nurses and Dr. Sam yelp with laughter.

I go home and collapse. I've got a fever and a splitting headache. I call my doctor, who (perplexed) orders antibiotics and a few days of rest. What I need is time to stop the motor and take a break. In a few days all my spare parts will be repaired and back to working order but for now I am feeling physically, mentally and emotionally diminished. It's out of the question to read, talk on the phone or even eat. I cannot imagine any damn clown coming in and turning off my T.V. to do his number. I'd kill him. How do those kids put up with us?

55.

"Something has changed here"

Mimi says, "Oh my god, there are dust storms and a hurricane warning. I want to head for the tropics." Me too. This is my last day before a long and needed summer break.

After hearing the weather report I am afraid that there is a child in danger of a trip to the stars, only to find out from an aide that the Queen Bee had come in at 8 A.M. to oversee the housekeeping and conduct a massive dust hunt. (It's a good thing that Nadine and I are tall enough to keep all the tops of our lockers sparkling.) False alarm. Still our nurses are in a tizzy.

Dora gives us the news with the daily list of children. She looks relaxed for a change, her nose peeling from having just come back from a week in the sun. "Something has changed lately here, the bosses are letting the kids roam the hallways more and more." (I wonder, when did it all start to change?) I don't get it, but I like it. We have a new protocol, kids can leave their rooms to play in the hallways and go home for weekends."

Dora continues: "One of the new kids will be 6 years old today; the one from an African family, our "enfant terrible." She's got a high fever. Separated from her twin brother for the first time, she has been in isolation for the last month without leaving her room; doesn't get many visits. When she is feeling well, she's uncontrollable, plays with the rules, tries every trick in the book and the nurses are at their wit's end. I told the volunteers not to leave scissors in that room after arts and crafts!" I want to investigate the situation.

While La Mouche fools around with Louie in the hallways, I go and find the kid in bed shaking with 103 degree temperature and no nurse, no mom, no auntie or no dad in sight. I see a jittery lump under the covers, an untouched piece of birthday cake on the bed table next to a solitary black pigtail that must have fallen off. She's almost bald now. I stay for 20 minutes, singing low key songs with one hand on her back. The trembling slows and the girl starts to ramble and chatter, saying that she could die if she leaves the room. I keep singing through her delirium. Am I staying too long in her room? I am getting bonded to this one and feel secretly relieved that I am cutting out today. I've had my fill of tattoos on the heart, lately.

Rosa arrives before lunch with her tall father. She has an appointment with the Professor who is worried about some swollen glands. She looks healthy to me, but her behaviour has changed. She has become so gentle and loving that all she wants are peaceful clowns. We do a number on her toy monkey (Booboo), sing it to sleep. Before leaving the hospital, Rosa presses a note into my palm: "Je t'aime." I am left to face my own emotions.

This afternoon, Diane is receiving a quart size bag of lifesaving bone marrow from her younger sister. We walk in just at the moment that the fluids begin to flow. I can't believe she is alone and trying to sleep during this important event. I suppose her family is with the sibling who must be waking up by now. Not wanting Diane to miss this moment, for better or for worse, La Mouche and I gently start singing. We fill the room with harmony as Diane smiles and looks dreamy. The marrow flows into her silently. I don't have the nerve to tell her I wouldn't be around for the next five weeks, that I need a serious break and ache to see something green again. I am empty yet I feel full to the brim. How dare I leave, when she is stuck growing new blood cells. I hope she will understand.

As I pack up my ears, white coat and props I can hear the kids giggling, running around in the hallways. In my absence La Mouche will carry on twice a week even though she teases me about abandoning her. So will the other clowns, the nurses, doctors and our dear Professor. Life goes on here, with or without me.

56.

Signature

I've come to my hideaway in the south of France where I feel safe. The nights are immense and quiet, only interrupted by the church bells. The shelves are full of delicious books to read. From my bedroom I can smell thyme, rosemary, lavender; here I can sleep late, gorge myself on goat cheese, swim in my blessed lake and forget the hospital. It's so difficult to get the children out of my mind.

"Ma petite Caro, Ophelia died of heart failure. (She follows her momma into the sky of the unforgotten.) It all was so sudden. We won't ever forget her.", writes Nadine in a letter. I take the time to realise and feel what she has just told me. After all, I am not in the hospital and don't have to perform all day for the kids. My red nose is tucked away in a costume trunk; I can allow myself the luxury of reflecting, musing. But I feel stuck in a void, without emotion. The letter continues, "Antoine's B.M.T. was a success. So was Diane's. She's got a new boyfriend who escorted her to the day clinic last week for a L.P. . Louie is doing fine, the rascal came by after his consultation with the Professor just to tease Loulou the Leek. Alice's hair is growing out, she's getting a new treatment and is finally showing signs of delightful irreverence. Our little African princess follows her everywhere, demanding attention and fairy tales. And that Martin, he gets rounder and cuter by the minute; keeps everyone laughing, including us! Mimi has gone to Mexico to get some sun. The nurses and the Queen Bee send their love."

I drive to the lake with a powerful need to float, dissolve if possible. The water is flawless, almost turquoise, no wind. Funny, I don't see birds today. Swimming far out to the middle, I have an irresistible urge to turn face down, open my eyes, stop breathing for ten long seconds. What would it feel like to let go, like Shakespeare's Ophelia, sinking into my grief? Belly down, I open my eyes and gaze into the unknown. For how long? Heavy-hearted, resolved to breathe again, I flip over to contemplate the open sky and take time to consider the last few months. Float some more and maybe let myself languish; let go of so many memories that spin out of control in my thoughts. I begin to feel weightless and lose track of time. A seagull appears from out of nowhere, flying circles above me, gliding, ascending with grace. Hot tears drip into the cool water.

The work I have chosen has taken it's toll on me; like an emotional roller coaster speeding high-up and low-down so many times that I cannot remember when life felt ordinary, even-keeled. Yet I am balanced; for it always felt so natural and fulfilling to create laughter and lose myself in play, in my clowning. Some days I forgot how many children survived illness and went on to live life fully. I still get letters and calls from them all the time to remind me. I look forward to Uncle Jack's calls! But after the loss of certain kids, or seeing the sorrow of parents and nurses, I felt slaughtered and reeling, incapable of getting out of bed, questioning the decency of our work. Most other times, when days at the hospital with my partner had generated moments of poetry or hilarity, I felt drunk with joy, full of purpose, sure of my path. I knew that it was all worth it; essential to put one foot in front of the other, to carry on. That little scrap of paper from Rosa is testimony, "Je t'aime." I keep it with me to remember.

*

     One day I came home with a lump in my throat, but realised after taking off my scarf that it was only a red nose still hanging faithfully around my neck. Plastic ruby on a giraffe's neck. An oversight, a stigmata? Like a scarlet beauty mark, it resonated with my identity, my difference, my link to humanity. My signature.

Le Rire Medecin clowns

Paris team
Dr. April, Alexis Armengol-Humbert
Madame Baden-Baden, Marion Clarac
Dr. Basket, Pierrette Bonnefont
Dr. Mephisto Balthazar, Ami Hattab
Dr. Bob, Yann Siprott
Dr. Amedee Chic, Dominique Langlais
Dr. Roger Chips, Jean Philippe Buzaud
Dr. Cauli-flower, Anne Vissuzaine
Dr. Pigtails, Margo McLaughlin
Dr. Babycakes, Bernie Collins
Dr. Frida Lekker, Pina Blaankvoort
Dr. Giraffe, Caroline Simonds
Dr. Coco-a-Gogo, Helene Gustin
Pr. Gusave, Guy Lafrance
Dr. Jeep, Lory Leshin
Dr. Josephine, Stephanie Liesenfeld
La Mouche, Nadine Demange
Mlle. Mauricette, Bernadette Coqueret
Loulou the Leek, Jean Louis Berdat
Pr. Pewpew, Philippe Aymard
Dr. Z'el, Emmanuelle Bon
Dr. Z'yva Zen, Alex Pavlata

Nantes team
Pr. Leonie, Odile Bouvais
Dr. Hervé, Tayeb Hassini
Dr. Moustique, Francoise Milet
Mme Muguette, Nathalie Tual
Dr. Poussin, Alain Pierre

Orleans team
Dr. Allumette Pochon, Nathalie Bauchet
Dr. Articho, Philippe Fauconnier
Dr. Pompom, Alain Hatton
Dr. Zaza Bonbec, Sophie Jude
Brancardier Nano, Vincent Pensuet

Code of Ethics
Le Rire Medecin

A non-profit organisation under Law 1901, enacted May 29, 1991 (No. 91-7886)

The Rire Médecin is composed of a team of artists. Working in close collaboration with medical careworkers, it creates regular performances for hospitalised children.

In order to maintain the quality and the professionalism of their *work - without limiting the creativity of the artists, it is necessary to formulate in a code of ethics the principles of Le Rire Médecin. Thus, any participation in the activities of Le Rire Médecin requires knowledge, acceptance and application of the fundamental principles expressed in this code.

*(The word "work" signifies the activities of the clowns in the hospital.)

Article 1
The artist who works in the hospital is a professional who has been hired and paid by Le Rire Médecin. He is trained and skilled in the performing arts and is experienced in this field. Le Rire Medecin provides training for working in a hospital in order for the artist to better understand and respect this environment and to assist him in adapting his skills.

Article 2
Inside the hospital, the artist will perform no function that is outside the boundaries of his artistic activities.
The artist is present in the hospital to help children and their families cope with hospitalisation. His work reveals that humour and fantasy can become part of hospital life. The artist must be aware that the purpose of his work is to improve the well-being not only of the children but also their families and the medical careworkers. The artist always proceeds with respect for the work of the medical teams and careworkers.

Article 3
The artist never works alone at the hospital. He works as part of a duet and is always accompanied by a partner.

Article 4
The artist is responsible for his actions inside the hospital.

The artist bases his work on respect for the dignity, the personality and the privacy of the child and his family.

The artist maintains the same professional integrity regardless of the patient's gender, nationality, race, religion, sexual orientation, traditions, family situation, social status, education, illness, or any feelings he may have about that person.

He will abstain from any and all remarks that could be inappropriate, even if his opinion is solicited. He will take care not to make any allusion to his own background, traditions, religious faith or political beliefs that could be harmful.

Article 5

The artist will respect the privacy of patients and their families and maintain professional discretion and confidentiality notwithstanding appropriate intercommunication with other medical careworkers. Confidential information includes anything that has been confided, but also what one has seen, read, heard, or understood concerning the patients' state of health. The artist will also not disclose the patients' identities or their medical records. Discretion is mandatory in all locations: inside as well as outside the hospital (elevators, dressing or locker rooms, and public places).

Article 6

No matter what the request, the artist will not enter into a relationship with the patient or his family outside of the artist's professional activities. He must never become the friend or confidante of the patient or family. In case of repeated solicitations on the part of the family, the artist must speak to a supervisor on the medical care team.

Article 7

To guarantee the quality of his work, the artist will maintain and perfect his artistic skills (clown techniques) as well as his theoretical knowledge (various pathologies, chow children cope with pain, medical vocabulary, child development, etc.).

Article 8

The artist is always vigilant concerning the patient's safety. Patients must not be endangered by the artist's activity, his props, or his movements.

Article 9

The artist respects the rules and regulations concerning hygiene and security specific to each ward in the hospital.

Article 10

The artist never takes sides concerning controversies within the hospital, complaints about service, or problems regarding personnel or management.

Article 11

In his capacity as a Rire Medecin worker, the artist will not accept any gratuities for his work and may not participate in any promotional activity or any commercial venture.

Copyright in Paris on February 13, 1995

To contact Le Rire Medecin:
18 rue Geoffroy L'Asnier
75004 Paris, France
www.leriremedecin.asso.fr